CAMBRIDGE LIBRARY COLLECTION

Books of enduring scholarly value

English Men of Letters

In the 1870s, Macmillan publishers began to issue a series of books called 'English Men of Letters' – biographies of English writers by other English writers. The general editor of the series was the journalist, critic, politician, and supporter (and later biographer) of Gladstone, John Morley (1838–1923). The aim was to provide a short introduction to each subject and his works, but also that the life should illuminate the works, and vice versa. The subjects range chronologically from Chaucer to Thackeray and Dickens, and an important feature of the series is that many of the authors (Henry James on Hawthorne, Ward on Dickens) were discussing writers of the previous generation, and some (Trollope on Thackeray) had even known their subjects personally. The series exemplifies the British approach to literary biography and criticism at the end of the nineteenth century, and also reveals which authors were at that time regarded as canonical.

Gibbon

Described by his biographer as the author of 'monumental and supreme' histories, Edward Gibbon (1737–94) is widely acknowledged as a major figure of the Enlightenment and the father of modern historical scholarship. However, despite these epithets, the personal life of one of the eighteenth century's most successful authors remains unknown to many of his readers. Published in the first series of English Men of Letters in 1878 (and going into a second edition in the same year), this biography by James Cotter Morison (1832–88) provides a learned but accessible account of the man who wrote *The Decline and Fall of the Roman Empire*. Starting with a childhood plagued by ill health and infirmity, and covering Gibbon's time in the militia and travelling on the Grand Tour, Morison leads readers through a life which was apparently unremarkable, but in fact resulted in a work of enduring scholarly achievement.

Cambridge University Press has long been a pioneer in the reissuing of out-of-print titles from its own backlist, producing digital reprints of books that are still sought after by scholars and students but could not be reprinted economically using traditional technology. The Cambridge Library Collection extends this activity to a wider range of books which are still of importance to researchers and professionals, either for the source material they contain, or as landmarks in the history of their academic discipline.

Drawing from the world-renowned collections in the Cambridge University Library, and guided by the advice of experts in each subject area, Cambridge University Press is using state-of-the-art scanning machines in its own Printing House to capture the content of each book selected for inclusion. The files are processed to give a consistently clear, crisp image, and the books finished to the high quality standard for which the Press is recognised around the world. The latest print-on-demand technology ensures that the books will remain available indefinitely, and that orders for single or multiple copies can quickly be supplied.

The Cambridge Library Collection will bring back to life books of enduring scholarly value (including out-of-copyright works originally issued by other publishers) across a wide range of disciplines in the humanities and social sciences and in science and technology.

Gibbon

James Cotter Morison

CAMBRIDGE
UNIVERSITY PRESS

CAMBRIDGE UNIVERSITY PRESS

Cambridge, New York, Melbourne, Madrid, Cape Town,
Singapore, São Paolo, Delhi, Tokyo, Mexico City

Published in the United States of America by Cambridge University Press, New York

www.cambridge.org
Information on this title: www.cambridge.org/9781108034685

This edition first published 1878
This digitally printed version 2011

ISBN 978-1-108-03468-5 Paperback

English Men of Letters

EDITED BY JOHN MORLEY

GIBBON

GIBBON

BY

JAMES COTTER MORISON, M.A.
LINCOLN COLLEGE, OXFORD.

SECOND EDITION.

London:
MACMILLAN AND CO.
1878.

LONDON :

R. CLAY, SONS, AND TAYLOR, PRINTERS

BREAD STREET HILL.

CONTENTS

CHAPTER VI.

CHAPTER VII.

CHAPTER VIII.

CHAPTER IX.

CHAPTER X.

GIBBON

GIBBON

CHAPTER I.

EDWARD GIBBON [1] was born at Putney, near London,
on 27th April in the year 1737. After the reformation
of the calendar his birthday became the 8th of May.
He was the eldest of a family of seven children ; but
his five brothers and only sister all died in early infancy,
and he could remember in after life his sister alone,
whom he also regretted.

He is at some pains in his Memoirs to show the
length and quality of his pedigree, which he traces back
to the times of the Second and Third Edwards. Noting
the fact, we pass on to a nearer ancestor, his grand-

---

[1] Gibbon's Memoirs and Letters are of such easy access that I
have not deemed it necessary to encumber these pages with references to them. Any one who wishes to control my statements will
have no difficulty in doing so with the Miscellaneous Works,
edited by Lord Sheffield, in his hand. Whenever I advance anything that seems to require corroboration, I have been careful to
give my authority.

father, who seems to have been a person of considerable
energy of character and business talent. He made a
large fortune, which he lost in the South-Sea Scheme,
and then made another before his death. He was
one of the Commissioners of Customs, and sat at the
Board with the poet Prior; Bolingbroke was heard to
declare that no man knew better than Mr. Edward
Gibbon the commerce and finances of England. His
son, the historian's father, was a person of very inferior
stamp. He was educated at Westminster and Cambridge, travelled on the Continent, sat in Parliament,
lived beyond his means as a country gentleman, and
here his achievements came to an end. He seems to
have been a kindly but a weak and impulsive man, who
however had the merit of obtaining and deserving his
son's affection by genial sympathy and kindly treatment.

Gibbon's childhood was passed in chronic illness,
debility, and disease. All attempts to give him a
regular education were frustrated by his precarious
health. The longest period he ever passed at school
were two years at Westminster, but he was constantly
moved from one school to another. This even his delicacy can hardly explain, and it must have been fatal
to all sustained study. Two facts he mentions of his
school life, which paint the manners of the age. In the
year 1746 such was the strength of party spirit that
he, a child of nine years of age, "was reviled and
buffeted for the sins of his Tory ancestors." Secondly,
the worthy pedagogues of that day found no readier
way of leading the most studious of boys to a love of
science than corporal punishment. "At the expense of
many tears and some blood I purchased the knowledge
of the Latin syntax." Whether all love of study would

have been flogged out of him if he had remained at
school, it is difficult to say, but it is not an improbable
supposition that this would have happened. The risk
was removed by his complete failure of health. "A
strange nervous affection, which alternately contracted
his legs and produced, without any visible symptom,
the most excruciating pain," was his chief affliction,
followed by intervals of languor and debility. The
saving of his life during these dangerous years Gibbon
unhesitatingly ascribes to the more than maternal care
of his aunt, Catherine Porten, on writing whose name
for the first time in his Memoirs, "he felt a tear of
gratitude trickling down his cheek." "If there be
any," he continues, "as I trust there are some, who
rejoice that I live, to that dear and excellent woman
they must hold themselves indebted. Many anxious
and solitary hours and days did she consume in the
patient trial of relief and amusement; many wakeful
nights did she sit by my bedside in trembling expectation
that every hour would be my last." Gibbon is rather
anxious to get over these details, and declares he has
no wish to expatiate on a "disgusting topic." This is
quite in the style of the *ancien régime*. There was
no blame attached to any one for being ill in those
days, but people were expected to keep their infirmities
to themselves. "People knew how to live and die in
those days, and kept their infirmities out of sight.
You might have the gout, but you must walk about all
the same without making grimaces. It was a point
of good breeding to hide one's sufferings."[1] Similarly Walpole was much offended by a too faithful
publication of Madame de Sévigné's *Letters*. "Heaven

[1] George Sand, quoted in Taine's *Ancien Régime*, p. 181.

forbid," he says, "that I should say that the letters
of Madame de Sévigné were bad. I only meant that
they were full of family details and mortal distempers,
to which the most immortal of us are subject." But
Gibbon was above all things a veracious historian, and
fortunately has not refrained from giving us a truthful
picture of his childhood.

Of his studies, or rather his reading—his early and
invincible love of reading, which he would not ex-
change for the treasures of India—he gives us a full
account, and we notice at once the interesting fact
that a considerable portion of the historical field afterwards occupied by his great work had been already
gone over by Gibbon before he was well in his teens.
"My indiscriminate appetite subsided by degrees into
the historic line, and since philosophy has exploded
all innate ideas and natural propensities, I must
ascribe the choice to the assiduous perusal of the
Universal History as the octavo volumes successively
appeared. This unequal work referred and introduced me to the Greek and Roman historians, to as
many at least as were accessible to an English reader.
All that I could find were greedily devoured, from
Littlebury's lame *Herodotus* to Spelman's valuable
Xenophon, to the pompous folios of Gordon's *Tacitus*,
and a ragged *Procopius* of the beginning of the last
century." Referring to an accident which threw the
continuation of Echard's *Roman History* in his way, he
says, "To me the reigns of the successors of Constantine were absolutely new, and I was immersed in
the passage of the Goths over the Danube, when the
summons of the dinner-bell reluctantly dragged me from
my intellectual feast. . . . I procured the second and

third volumes of Howell's *History of the World*, which
exhibit the Byzantine period on a larger scale. Mahomet
and his Saracens soon fixed my attention, and some
instinct of criticism directed me to the genuine sources.
Simon Ockley first opened my eyes, and I was led
from one book to another till I had ranged round the
circle of Oriental history. Before I was sixteen I had
exhausted all that could be learned in English of the
Arabs and Persians, the Tartars and Turks, and the
same ardour urged me to guess at the French of
D'Herbelot and to construe the barbarous Latin of
Pocock's *Abulfaragius.*" Here is in rough outline a
large portion at least of the *Decline and Fall* already
surveyed. The fact shows how deep was the sympathy
that Gibbon had for his subject, and that there was a
sort of pre-established harmony between his mind and
the historical period he afterwards illustrated.

Up to the age of fourteen it seemed that Gibbon,
as he says, was destined to remain through life an
illiterate cripple. But as he approached his sixteenth
year, a great change took place in his constitution, and
his diseases, instead of growing with his growth and
strengthening with his strength, wonderfully vanished.
This unexpected recovery was not seized by his father
in a rational spirit, as affording a welcome opportunity
of repairing the defects of a hitherto imperfect education. Instead of using the occasion thus presented of
recovering some of the precious time lost, of laying a
sound foundation of scholarship and learning on which
a superstructure at the university or elsewhere could
be ultimately built, he carried the lad off in an impulse
of perplexity and impatience, and entered him as a
gentleman commoner at Magdalen College just before he

had completed his fifteenth year (1752, April 3). This
was perhaps the most unwise step he could have taken
under the circumstances. Gibbon was too young and
too ignorant to profit by the advantages offered by Oxford
to a more mature student, and his status as a gentleman
commoner seemed intended to class him among the idle
and dissipated who are only expected to waste their
money and their time. A good education is generally
considered as reflecting no small credit on its possessor;
but in the majority of cases it reflects credit on the
wise solicitude of his parents or guardians rather than
on himself. If Gibbon escaped the peril of being an
ignorant and frivolous lounger, the merit was his own.

At no period in their history had the English universities sunk to a lower condition as places of education
than at the time when Gibbon went up to Oxford.
To speak of them as seats of learning seems like irony;
they were seats of nothing but coarse living and clown-
ish manners, the centres where all the faction, party
spirit, and bigotry of the country were gathered to a head.
In this evil pre-eminence both of the universities and
all the colleges appear to have been upon a level, though
Lincoln College, Oxford, is mentioned as a bright exception in John Wesley's day to the prevalent degeneracy.
The strange thing is that, with all their neglect of
learning and morality, the colleges were not the resorts
of jovial if unseemly boon companionship; they were
collections of quarrelsome and spiteful litigants, who
spent their time in angry lawsuits. The indecent con-
tentions between Bentley and the Fellows of Trinity
were no isolated scandal. They are best known and
remembered on account of the eminence of the chief
disputants, and of the melancholy waste of Bentley's

genius which they occasioned. Hearne writes of Oxford
in 1726, "There are such differences now in the University of Oxford (hardly one college but where all the
members are busied in law business and quarrels not
at all relating to the promotion of learning), that good
letters decay every day, insomuch that this ordination
on Trinity Sunday at Oxford there were no fewer (as I
am informed) than fifteen denied orders for insufficiency,
which is the more to be noted because our bishops,
and those employed by them, are themselves illiterate
men."[1]   The state of things had not much improved
twenty or thirty years later when Gibbon went up, but
perhaps it had improved a little.   He does not mention
lawsuits as a favourite pastime of the Fellows.   "The
Fellows or monks of my time," he says, "were decent,
easy men, who supinely enjoyed the gifts of the founder :
their days were filled by a series of uniform employ-
ments—the chapel, the hall, the coffee-house, and the
common room—till they retired weary and well satisfied
to a long slumber.   From the toil of reading, writing,
or thinking they had absolved their consciences.   Their
conversation stagnated in a round of college business,
Tory politics, personal anecdotes, and private scandal.
Their dull and deep potations excused the brisk intemperance of youth, and their constitutional toasts were
not expressive of the most lively loyalty to the House
of Hanover."   Some Oxonians perhaps could still partly
realise the truth of this original picture by their recollections of faint and feeble copies of it drawn from
their experience in youthful days.   It seems to be certain that the universities, far from setting a model of

[1] *Social Life at the English Universities.* By Christopher
Wordsworth. Page 57.

good living, were really below the average standard of
the morals and manners of the age, and the standard was
not high. Such a satire as the *Terræ Filius* of Amhurst
cannot be accepted without large deductions; but the
caricaturist is compelled by the conditions of his craft
to aim at the *true seeming*, if he neglects the true, and
with the benefit of this limitation the *Terræ Filius*
reveals a deplorable and revolting picture of vulgarity,
insolence, and licence. The universities are spoken of
in terms of disparagement by men of all classes. Lord
Chesterfield speaks of the "rust" of Cambridge as
something of which a polished man should promptly rid
himself. Adam Smith showed his sense of the defects
of Oxford in a stern section of the *Wealth of Nations*,
written twenty years after he had left the place. Even
youths like Gray and West, fresh from Eton, express
themselves with contempt for their respective universities. "Consider me," says the latter, writing from
Christ Church, "very seriously, here is a strange country,
inhabited by things that call themselves Doctors and
Masters of Arts, a country flowing with syllogisms and
ale; where Horace and Virgil are equally unknown."
Gray, answering from Peterhouse, can only do justice
to his feelings by quoting the words of the Hebrew
prophet, and insists that Isaiah had Cambridge
equally with Babylon in view when he spoke of
the wild beasts and wild asses, of the satyrs that
dance, of an inhabitation of dragons and a court for
owls.

Into such untoward company was Gibbon thrust by
his careless father at the age of fifteen. That he succumbed to the unwholesome atmosphere cannot surprise
us. He does not conceal, perhaps he rather exaggerates,

in his Memoirs, the depth of his fall. As Bunyan in
a state of grace accused himself of dreadful sins which
in all likelihood he never committed, so it is probable
that Gibbon, in his old age, when study and learning
were the only passions he knew, reflected with too much
severity on the boyish freaks of his university life.
Moreover there appears to have been nothing coarse
or unworthy in his dissipation; he was simply idle.
He justly lays much of the blame on the authorities.
To say that the discipline was lax would be to pay
it an unmerited compliment. There was no discipline
at all. He lived in Magdalen as he might have
lived at the Angel or the Mitre Tavern. He not
only left his college, but he left the university, whenever he liked. In one winter he made a tour to
Bath, another to Buckinghamshire, and he made four
excursions to London, "without once hearing the voice
of admonition, without once feeling the hand of control." Of study he had just as much and as little as he
pleased.

"As soon as my tutor had sounded the insufficiency
of his disciple in school learning, he proposed that we
should read every morning from ten to eleven the
comedies of Terence. During the first weeks I constantly attended these lessons in my tutor's room; but
as they appeared equally devoid of profit and pleasure,
I was once tempted to try the experiment of a formal
apology. The apology was accepted with a smile. I
repeated the offence with less ceremony: the excuse was
admitted with the same indulgence; the slightest motive
of laziness or indisposition, the most trifling avocation
at home or abroad was allowed as a worthy impediment,
nor did my tutor appear conscious of my absence or

neglect." No wonder he spoke with indignation of such scandalous neglect. "To the University of Oxford," he says, "I acknowledge no obligation, and she will as readily renounce me for a son, as I am willing to disclaim her for a mother. I spent fourteen months at Magdalen College; they proved the most idle and unprofitable of my whole life. The reader will pronounce between the school and the scholar." This is only just and fully merited by the abuses denounced. One appreciates the anguish of the true scholar mourning over lost time as a miser over lost gold. There was another side of the question which naturally did not occur to Gibbon, but which may properly occur to us. Did Gibbon lose as much as he thought in missing the scholastic drill of the regular public school and university man? Something he undoubtedly lost: he was never a finished scholar, up to the standard even of his own day. If he had been, is it certain that the accomplishment would have been all gain? It may be doubted. At a later period Gibbon read the classics with the free and eager curiosity of a thoughtful mind. It was a labour of love, of passionate ardour, similar to the manly zeal of the great scholars of the Renaissance. This appetite had not been blunted by enforced toil in a prescribed groove. How much of that zest for antiquity, of that keen relish for the classic writers which he afterwards acquired and retained through life, might have been quenched if he had first made their acquaintance as school-books? Above all, would he have looked on the ancient world with such freedom and originality as he afterwards gained, if he had worn through youth the harness of academical study? These questions do not suggest an answer, but they may furnish a doubt.

Oxford and Cambridge for nearly a century have been
turning out crowds of thorough-paced scholars of the
orthodox pattern. It is odd that the two greatest historians who have been scholars as well—Gibbon and
Grote—were not university-bred men.

As if to prove by experiment where the fault lay, in
" the school or the scholar," Gibbon had no sooner left
Oxford for the long vacation, than his taste for study
returned, and, not content with readirg, he attempted
original composition. The subject he selected was a
curious one for a youth in his sixteenth year. It was
an attempt to settle the chronology of the age of Sesostris, and shows how soon the austere side of history had
attracted his attention. " In my childish balance," he
says, " I presumed to weigh the systems of Scaliger and
Petavius, of Marsham and of Newton; and my sleep
has been disturbed by the difficulty of reconciling the
Septuagint with the Hebrew computation." Of course
his essay had the usual value of such juvenile productions; that is, none at all, except as an indication of
early bias to serious study of history. On his return
to Oxford, the age of Sesostris was wisely relinquished.
He indeed soon commenced a line of study which was
destined to have a lasting influence on the remainder of
his course through life.

He had an inborn taste for theology and the controversies which have arisen concerning religious dogma.
" From my childhood," he says, " I had been fond cf
religious disputation : my poor aunt has often been
puzzled by the mysteries which she strove to believe."
How he carried the taste into mature life, his great
chapters on the heresies and controversies of the
Early Church are there to show. This inclination for

theology, co-existing with a very different temper towards religious sentiment, recalls the similar case of the
author of the *Historical and Critical Dictionary*, the
illustrious Pierre Bayle, whom Gibbon resembled in
more ways than one.   At Oxford his religous education,
like everything else connected with culture, had been
entirely neglected.   It seems hardly credible, yet we
have his word for it, that he never subscribed or
studied the Articles of the Church of England, and
was never confirmed.   When he first went up, he was
judged to be too young, but the Vice-Chancellor
directed him to return as soon as he had completed
his fifteenth year, recommending him in the meantime
to the instruction of his college.   " My college forgot
to instruct ; I forgot to return, and was myself forgotten by the first magistrate of the university.   Without a single lecture, either public or private, either
Christian or Protestant, without any academical sub-
scription, without any episcopal ordination, I was left
by light of my catechism to grope my way to the
chapel and communion table, where I was admitted
without question how far or by what means I might
be qualified to receive the sacrament.   Such almost incredible neglect was productive of the worst mischiefs."
What did Gibbon mean by this last sentence ?   Did he,
when he wrote it, towards the end of his life, regret
the want of early religious instruction ?   Nothing leads
us to think so, or to suppose that his subsequent loss of
faith was a heavy grief, supported, but painful to bear.
His mind was by nature positive, or even pagan, and he
had nothing of what the Germans call *religiosität* in
him.   Still there is a passage in his Memoirs where
he oddly enough laments not having selected the *fat*

slumbers of the Church as an eligible profession. Did
he reflect that perhaps the neglect of his religious education at Oxford had deprived him of a bishopric or a good
deanery, and the learned leisure which such positions
at that time conferred on those who cared for it? He
could not feel that he was morally, or even spiritually,
unfit for an office filled in his own time by such men
as Warburton and Hurd. He would not have disgraced
the episcopal bench; he would have been dignified,
courteous, and hospitable; a patron and promoter of
learning, we may be sure. His literary labours would
probably have consisted of an edition of a Greek play
or two, and certainly some treatise on the Evidences of
Christianity. But in that case we should not have had
the *Decline and Fall*.

The "blind activity of idleness" to which he was
exposed at Oxford, prevented any result of this kind.
For want of anything better to do, he was led to read
Middleton's *Free Enquiry into the Miraculous Powers
which are Supposed to have Subsisted in the Christian
Church.* Gibbon says that the effect of Middleton's
"bold criticism" upon him was singular, and that
instead of making him a sceptic, it made him more of
a believer. He might have reflected that it is the
commonest of occurrences for controversialists to produce exactly the opposite result to that which they
intend, and that as many an apology for Christianity
has sown the first seeds of infidelity, so an attack upon
it might well intensify faith. What follows is very
curious. "The elegance of style and freedom of argument were repelled by a shield of prejudice. I still
revered the character, or rather the names of the saints
and fathers whom Dr. Middleton exposes; nor could he

destroy my implicit belief that the gift of miraculous
powers was continued in the Church during the first
four or five centuries of Christianity. But I was un-
able to resist the weight of historical evidence, that
within the same period most of the leading doctrines of
Popery were already introduced in theory and practice.
Nor was my conclusion absurd that miracles are the
test of truth, and that the Church must be orthodox
and pure which was so often approved by the visible
interposition of the Deity. The marvellous tales which
are boldly attested by the Basils and Chrysostoms, the
Austins and Jeromes, compelled me to embrace the superior merits of celibacy, the institution of the monastic
life, the use of the sign of the cross, of holy oil, and
even of images, the invocation of saints, the worship of
relics, the rudiments of purgatory in prayers for the
dead, and the tremendous mystery of the sacrifice of
the body and the blood of Christ, which insensibly
swelled into the prodigy of transubstantiation." In this
remarkable passage we have a distinct foreshadow of
the Tractarian movement, which came seventy or eighty
years afterwards. Gibbon in 1752, at the age of fifteen,
took up a position practically the same as Froude and
Newman took up about the year 1830. In other words,
he reached the famous *via media* at a bound. But a
second spring soon carried him clear of it, into the
bosom of the Church of Rome.

He had come to what are now called Church principles, by the energy of his own mind working on the
scanty data furnished him by Middleton. By one of
those accidents which usually happen in such cases, he
made the acquaintance of a young gentleman who
had already embraced Catholicism, and who was well

provided with controversial tracts in favour of Romanism. Among these were the two works of Bossuet, the
Exposition of Catholic Doctrine and the *History of the
Protestant Variations.* Gibbon says : "I read, I applauded, I believed, and surely I fell by a noble hand.
I have since examined the originals with a more discerning eye, and shall not hesitate to pronounce that Bossuet
is indeed a master of all the weapons of controversy.
In the *Exposition*, a specious apology, the orator assumes
with consummate art the tone of candour and simplicity, and the ten-horned monster is transformed at his
magic touch into the milk-white hind, who must be
loved as soon as she is seen. In the *History*, a bold
and well-aimed attack, he displays, with a happy mixture of narrative and argument, the faults and follies,
the changes and contradictions of our first Reformers,
whose variations, as he dexterously contends, are the
mark of historical error, while the perpetual unity of
the Catholic Church is the sign and test of infallible
truth. To my present feelings it seems incredible that I
should ever believe that I believed in transubstantiation.
But my conqueror oppressed me with the sacramental
words, '*Hoc est corpus meum*,' and dashed against each
other the figurative half meanings of the Protestant
sects ; every objection was resolved into omnipotence,
and, after repeating at St. Mary's the Athanasian
Creed, I humbly acquiesced in the mystery of the
Real Presence."

Many reflections are suggested on the respective
domains of reason and faith by these words, but they
cannot be enlarged on here. No one, nowadays, one
may hope, would think of making Gibbon's conversion
a subject of reproach to him. The danger is rather that

it should be regarded with too much honour. It unquestionably shows the early and trenchant force of his
intellect : he mastered the logical position in a moment;
saw the necessity of a criterion of faith ; and being told
that it was to be found in the practice of antiquity, boldly
went there, and abided by the result. But this praise
to his head does not extend to his heart. A more tender
and deep moral nature would not have moved so rapidly.
We must in fairness remember that it was not his fault
that his religious education had been neglected at home,
at school, and at college. But we have no reason to
think that had it been attended to, the result would
have been much otherwise. The root of spiritual life
did not exist in him. It never withered, because it never
shot up. Thus when he applied his acute mind to a
religious problem, he contemplated it with the coolness
and impartiality of a geometer or chess player, his
intellect operated *in vacuo* so to speak, untrammelled
by any bias of sentiment or early training. He had
no profound associations to tear out of his heart. He
merely altered the premisses of a syllogism. When
Catholicism was presented to him in a logical form, it
met with no inward bar and repugnance. The house
was empty and ready for a new guest, or rather the
first guest. If Gibbon anticipated the Tractarian movement intellectually, he was farther removed than the
poles are asunder from the mystic reverent spirit which
inspired that movement. If we read the *Apologia* of
Dr. Newman, we perceive the likeness and unlikeness of
the two cases. "As a matter of simple conscience," says
the latter, " I felt it to be a duty to protest against
the Church of Rome." At the time he refers to Dr.
Newman was a Catholic to a degree Gibbon never

dreamed of. But in the one case conscience and heart-
ties "strong as life, stronger almost than death,"
arrested the conclusions of the intellect. Ground which
Gibbon dashed over in a few months or weeks, the
great Tractarian took ten years to traverse. So different
is the mystic from the positive mind.

Gibbon had no sooner settled his new religion than
he resolved with a frankness which did him all honour
to profess it publicly. He wrote to his father, announc-
ing his conversion, a letter which he afterwards described, when his sentiments had undergone a complete
change, as written with all the pomp, dignity, and self-
satisfaction of a martyr. A momentary glow of enthusiasm had raised him, as he said, above all worldly considerations. He had no difficulty, in an excursion to
London, in finding a priest, who perceived in the first interview that persuasion was needless. "After sounding
the motives and merits of my conversion, he consented
to admit me into the pale of the Church, and at his feet
on the 8th of June 1753, I solemnly, though privately,
abjured the errors of heresy." He was exactly fifteen
years and one month old. Further details, which one
would like to have, he does not give. The scene even
of the solemn act is not mentioned, nor whether
he was baptized again; but this may be taken for
granted.

The fact of any one "going over to Rome" is too
common an occurrence nowadays to attract notice. But
in the eighteenth century it was a rare and startling
phenomenon. Gibbon's father, who was "neither a
bigot nor a philosopher," was shocked and astonished
by his "son's strange departure from the religion of his

C

country." He divulged the secret of young Gibbon's
conversion, and " the gates of Magdalen College were for
ever shut " against the latter's return. They really
needed no shutting at all. By the fact of his conversion to Romanism he had ceased to be a member
of the University.

CHAPTER II.

THE elder Gibbon showed a decision of character and prompt energy in dealing with his son's conversion to Romanism, which were by no means habitual with him. He swiftly determined to send him out of the country, far away from the influences and connections which had done such harm. Lausanne in Switzerland was the place selected for his exile, in which it was resolved he should spend some years in wholesome reflections on the error he had committed in yielding to the fascinations of Roman Catholic polemics. No time was lost : Gibbon had been received into the Church on the 8th of June, 1753, and on the 30th of the same month he had reached his destination. He was placed under the care of a M. Pavillard, a Calvinist minister, who had two duties laid upon him, a general one, to superintend the young man's studies, a particular and more urgent one, to bring him back to the Protestant faith.

It was a severe trial which Gibbon had now to undergo. He was by nature shy and retiring ; he was ignorant of French ; he was very young ; and with these disadvantages he was thrown among entire strangers alone. After the excitement and novelty of foreign travel were

c 2

over, and he could realise his position, he felt his heart
sink within him. From the luxury and freedom of
Oxford he was degraded to the dependence of a schoolboy. Pavillard managed his expenses, and his supply
of pocket-money was reduced to a small monthly allowance. " I had exchanged," he says, "my elegant apartment in Magdalen College for a narrow gloomy street, the
most unfrequented in an unhandsome town, for an old
inconvenient house, and for a small chamber ill-contrived
and ill-furnished, which on the approach of winter,
instead of a companionable fire, must be warmed by the
dull and invisible heat of a stove." Under these
gloomy auspices he began the most profitable, and after
a time the most pleasant, period of his whole life, one
on which he never ceased to look back with unmingled
satisfaction as the starting-point of his studies and intellectual progress.

The first care of his preceptor was to bring about his
religious conversion. Gibbon showed an honourable
tenacity to his new faith, and a whole year after he had
been exposed to the Protestant dialectics of Pavillard
he still, as the latter observed with much regret, continued to abstain from meat on Fridays. There is something slightly incongruous in the idea of Gibbon *fasting*
out of religious scruples, but the fact shows that his
religion had obtained no slight hold of him, and that
although he had embraced it quickly, he also accepted
with intrepid frankness all its consequences. His was
not an intellect that could endure half measures and
half lights ; he did not belong to that class of persons
who do not know their own minds.

However it is not surprising that his religion, placed
where he was, was slowly but steadily undermined. The

Swiss clergy, he says, were acute and learned on the topics
of controversy, and Pavillard seems to have been a good
specimen of his class. An adult and able man, in daily
contact with a youth in his own house, urging per-
sistently but with tact one side of a thesis, could hardly
fail in the course of time to carry his point. But though
Gibbon is willing to allow his tutor a handsome share
in the work of his conversion, he maintains that it was
chiefly effected by his own private reflections. And this
is eminently probable. What logic had set up, logic
could throw down. He gives us a highly characteristic
example of the reflections in question. "I still remember my solitary transport at the discovery of a philosophical argument against the doctrine of transubstantiation : that the text of Scripture which seems to inculcate
the Real Presence is attested only by a single sense—our
sight ; while the real presence itself is disproved by
three of our senses—the sight, the touch, and the taste."
He was unaware of the distinction between the logical
understanding and the higher reason, which has been
made since his time to the great comfort of thinkers of
a certain stamp. Having reached so far, his progress
was easy and rapid. "The various articles of the Romish
creed disappeared like a dream, and after a full conviction, on Christmas-day, 1754, I received the sacrament
in the church of Lausanne. It was here that I suspended
my religious inquiries, acquiescing with implicit belief
in the tenets and mysteries which are adopted by the
general consent of Catholics and Protestants." He thus
had been a Catholic for about eighteen months.

Gibbon's residence at Lausanne was a memorable
epoch in his life on two grounds. Firstly, it was during
the five years he spent there that he laid the founda-

tions of that deep and extensive learning by which he
was afterwards distinguished. Secondly, the foreign
education he there received, at the critical period when
the youth passes into the man, gave a permanent bent
to his mind, and made him a continental European
rather than an insular Englishman—two highly important factors in his intellectual growth.

He says that he went up to Oxford with a "stock of
erudition which might have puzzled a doctor, and a
degree of ignorance of which a schoolboy might have
been ashamed." Both erudition and ignorance were left
pretty well undisturbed during his short and ill-starred
university career. At Lausanne he found himself, for
the first time, in possession of the means of successful
study, good health, calm, books, and tuition, up to a
certain point : that point did not reach very far. The
good Pavillard, an excellent man, for whom Gibbon ever
entertained a sincere regard, was quite unequal to the
task of forming such a mind. There is no evidence that
he was a ripe or even a fair scholar, and the plain fact
is that Gibbon belongs to the honourable band of self-
taught men. "My tutor," says Gibbon, "had the good
sense to discern how far he could be useful, and when he
felt that I advanced beyond his speed and measure, he
wisely left me to my genius." Under that good guid-
ance he formed an extensive plan of reviewing the Latin
classics, in the four divisions of (1) Historians, (2) Poets,
(3) Orators, and (4) Philosophers, in "chronological
series from the days of Plautus and Sallust to the decline
of the language and empire of Rome." In one year he
read over the following authors : Virgil, Sallust, Livy,
Velleius Paterculus, Valerius Maximus, Tacitus, Sue-
tonius, Quintus Curtius, Justin, Florus, Plautus, Terence,

and Lucretius. We may take his word when he says that
this review, however rapid, was neither hasty nor superficial. Gibbon had the root of all scholarship in him,
the most diligent accuracy and an unlimited faculty of
taking pains. But he was a great scholar, not a minute
one, and belonged to the robust race of the Scaligers and
the Bentleys, rather than to the smaller breed of the
Elmsleys and Monks, and of course he was at no time
a professed philologer, occupied chiefly with the niceties
of language. The point which deserves notice in this
account of his studies is their wide sweep, so superior
and bracing, as compared with that narrow restric-
tion to the "authors of the best period," patronised
by teachers who imperfectly comprehend their own
business. Gibbon proceeded on the common-sense
principle, that if you want to obtain a real grasp of the
literature, history, and genius of a people, you must
master that literature with more or less completeness
from end to end, and that to select arbitrarily the
authors of a short period on the grounds that they are
models of style, is nothing short of foolish. It was the
principle on which Joseph Scaliger studied Greek, and
indeed occurs spontaneously to a vigorous mind eager for
real knowledge.[1]

Nor did he confine himself to reading : he felt that no
one is sure of knowing a language who limits his study
of it to the perusal of authors. He practised diligently
Latin prose composition, and this in the simplest and

[1] Vix delibatis conjugationibus Græcis, Homerum cum interpre-
tatione arreptum uno et viginti diebus totum didici. Reliquos vero
poetas Græcos omnes intra quatuor menses devoravi. Neque
ullum oratorem aut historicum prius attigi quam poetas omnes
tenerem.—*Scaligeri Epistolæ, Lib.* 1. *Epis.* 1.

most effectual way   " I translated an epistle of Cicero
into French, and after throwing it aside till the words
and phrases were obliterated from my memory, I re-
translated my French into such Latin as I could find,
and then compared each sentence of my imperfect version
with the ease, the grace, the propriety of the Roman
orator "   The only odd thing in connection with this
excellent method is that Gibbon in his Memoirs seems
to think it was a novel discovery of his own, and would
recommend it to the imitation of students, whereas it is
as old as the days of Ascham at least.   There is no indication that he ever in the least degree attempted Latin
verse, and it is improbable that he should have done so,
reading alone in Lausanne, under the slight supervision
of such a teacher as Pavillard.   The lack of this elegant
frivolity will be less thought of now than it would some
years ago.   But we may admit that it would have been
interesting to have a copy of hexameters or elegiacs by
the historian of Rome.   So much for Latin.   In Greek
he made far less progress.   He had attained his nineteenth year before he learned the alphabet, and even
after so late a beginning he did not prosecute the study
with much energy.

M. Pavillard seems to have taught him little more
than the rudiments.   " After my tutor had left me to
myself I worked my way through about half the *Iliad*,
and afterwards interpreted alone a large portion of Xenophon and Herodotus.   But my ardour, destitute of aid
and emulation, gradually cooled, and from the barren
task of searching words in a lexicon I withdrew to the
free and familiar conversation of Virgil and Tacitus."
This statement of the Memoirs is more than confirmed by
the journal of his studies, where we find him, as late as the

year 1762, when he was twenty-five years of age, painfully
reading Homer, it would appear, for the first time. He
read on an average about a book a week, and when he
had finished the *Iliad* this is what he says : " I have so
far met with the success I hoped for, that I have acquired
a great facility in reading the language, and treasured
up a very great stock of words. What I have rather
neglected is the grammatical construction of them, and
especially the many various inflections of the verbs."
To repair this defect he wisely resolved to bestow some
time every morning on the perusal of the Greek Grammar
of Port Royal. Thus we see that at an age when many
men are beginning to forget their Greek, Gibbon was
beginning to learn it. Was this early deficiency ever
repaired in Greek as it was in Latin ? I think not.
He never was at home in old Hellas as he was in old
Rome. This may be inferred from the discursive notes
of his great work, in which he has with admirable
skill incorporated so much of his vast and miscellaneous
reading. But his references to classic Greek authors are
relatively few and timid compared with his grasp and
mastery of the Latin. His judgments on Greek authors
are also, to say the least, singular. When he had
achieved the *Decline and Fall*, and was writing his
Memoirs in the last years of his life, the Greek writer
whom he selects for especial commendation is Xenophon.
" Cicero in Latin and Xenophon in Greek are indeed
the two ancients whom I would first propose to a liberal
scholar, not only for the merit of their style and sentiments, but for the admirable lessons which may be
applied almost to every situation of public and private
life." Of the merit of Xenophon's sentiments, most
people would now admit that the less said the better.

The warmth of Gibbon's language with regard to Xenophon contrasts with the coldness he shows with regard to Plato. " I involved myself," he says, "in the philosophic maze of the writings of Plato, of which perhaps the dramatic is more interesting than the argumentative part." That Gibbon knew amply sufficient Greek for his purposes as an historian no one doubts, but his honourable candour enables us to see that he was never a Greek scholar in the proper sense of the word.

It would be greatly to misknow Gibbon to suppose that his studies at Lausanne were restricted to the learned languages. He obtained something more than an elementary knowledge of mathematics, mastered De Crousaz' *Logic* and Locke's *Essay*, and filled up his spare time with that wide and discursive reading to which his boundless curiosity was always pushing him. He was thoroughly happy and contented, and never ceased throughout his life to congratulate himself on the fortunate exile which had placed him at Lausanne. In one respect he did not use his opportunities while in Switzerland. He never climbed a mountain all the time he was there, though he lived to see in his later life the first commencement of the Alpine fever. On the other hand, as became a historian and man of sense, the social and political aspects of the country engaged his attention, as well they might. He enjoyed access to the best society of the place, and the impression he made seems to have been as favourable as the one he received.

The influence of a foreign training is very marked in Gibbon, affecting as it does his general cast of thought, and even his style. It would be difficult to name any writer in our language, especially among the few who deserve to be compared with him, who is so un-English,

not in a bad sense of the word, as implying objection-
able qualities, but as wanting the clear insular stamp
and native flavour. If an intelligent Chinese or Persian
were to read his book in a French translation, he would
not readily guess that it was written by an Englishman.
It really bears the imprint of no nationality, and is
emphatically European. We may postpone the question
whether this is a merit or a defect, but it is a characteristic. The result has certainly been that he is one of
the best-known of English prose writers on the Continent, and one whom foreigners most readily comprehend.
This peculiarity, of which he himself was fully aware,
we may agree with him in ascribing to his residence
at Lausanne. At the 'flexible age of sixteen he soon
learned to endure, and gradually to adopt," foreign
manners. French became the language in which he
spontaneously thought; "his views were enlarged, and
his prejudices were corrected." In one particular he
cannot be complimented on the effect of his continental
education, when he congratulates himself "that his taste
for the French theatre had abated his idolatry for the
gigantic genius of Shakespeare, which is inculcated from
our infancy as the first duty of Englishmen." Still it
is well to be rid of idolatry and bigotry even with
regard to Shakespeare. We must remember that the
insular prejudices from which Gibbon rejoiced to be free
were very different in their intensity and narrowness
from anything of the kind which exists now. The
mixed hatred and contempt for foreigners which prevailed in his day, were enough to excite disgust in any
liberal mind.

The lucid order and admirable literary form of
Gibbon's great work are qualities which can escape no

observant reader. But they are qualities which are not
common in English books. The French have a saying,
"Les Anglais ne savent pas faire un livre." This is
unjust, taken absolutely, but as a general rule it is not
without foundation. It is not a question of depth or
originality of thought, nor of the various merits be-
longing to style properly so-called. In these respects
English authors need not fear competition. But in the
art of clear and logical arrangement, of building up
a book in such order and method that each part con-
tributes to the general effect of the whole, we must
own that we have many lessons to learn of our neighbours. Now in this quality Gibbon is a Frenchman.
Not Voltaire himself is more perspicuous than Gibbon.
Everything is in its place, and disposed in such apparently natural sequence that the uninitiated are apt to
think the matter could not have been managed otherwise. It is a case, if there ever was one, of consummate
art concealing every trace, not only of art, but even of
effort. Of course the grasp and penetrating insight
which are implied here, were part of Gibbon's great
endowment, which only Nature could give. But it was
fortunate that his genius was educated in the best
school for bringing out its innate quality.

   It would be difficult to explain why, except on that
principle of decimation by which Macaulay accounted
for the outcry against Lord Byron, Gibbon's solitary and
innocent love passage has been made the theme of a good
deal of malicious comment. The parties most interested,
and who, we may presume, knew the circumstances
better than any one else, seem to have been quite satisfied with each other's conduct. Gibbon and Mdlle.
Curchod, afterwards Madame Necker, remained on

terms of the *most* intimate friendship till the end of the
former's life. This might be supposed sufficient. But
it has not been so considered by evil tongues. The
merits of the case, however, may be more conveniently
discussed in a later chapter. At this point it will be
enough to give the facts.

Mdlle. Susanne Curchod was born about the year
1740; her father was the Calvinist minister of Crassier,
her mother a French Huguenot who had preferred her
religion to her country. She had received a liberal and
even learned education from her father, and was as
attractive in person as she was accomplished in mind.
" She was beautiful with that pure virginal beauty which
depends on early youth" (Sainte-Beuve). In 1757 she
was the talk of Lausanne, and could not appear in an
assembly or at the play without being surrounded by
admirers; she was called La Belle Curchod. Gibbon's
curiosity was piqued to see such a prodigy, and he was
smitten with love at first sight. "I found her" he says
"learned without pedantry, lively in conversation, pure in
sentiment, and elegant in manners." He was twenty and
she seventeen years of age; no impediment was placed
in the way of their meeting; and he was a frequent
guest in her father's house. In fact Gibbon paid his
court with an assiduity which makes an exception in his
usually unromantic nature. "She listened," he says,
"to the voice of truth and passion, and I might presume to hope that I had made some impression on a
virtuous heart." We must remember that this and
other rather glowing passages in his Memoirs were
written in his old age, when he had returned to Lausanne, and when, after a long separation and many
vicissitudes, he and Madame Necker were again thrown

together in an intimacy of friendship which revived old
memories. Letters of hers to him which will be quoted
in a later chapter show this in a striking light. He
indulged, he says, his dream of felicity, but on his
return to England he soon discovered that his father
would not hear of this "strange alliance," and then
follows the sentence which has lost him in the eyes of
some persons. "After a painful struggle I yielded to my
fate : I sighed as a lover, I obeyed as a son." What
else he was to do under the circumstances does not
appear. He was wholly dependent on his father, and
on the Continent at least parental authority is not
regarded as a trifling impediment in such cases. Gibbon
could only have married Mdlle. Curchod as an exile and
a pauper, if he had openly withstood his father's wishes.
"All for love" is a very pretty maxim, but it is apt to
entail trouble when practically applied. Jean-Jacques
Rousseau, who had the most beautiful sentiments on
paper, but who in real life was not always a model of
self-denial, found, as we shall see, grave fault with
Gibbon's conduct. Gibbon, as a plain man of rather
prosaic good sense, behaved neither heroically nor
meanly. Time, absence, and the scenes of a new life,
which he found in England, had their usual effect ; his
passion vanished. "My cure," he says, "was accelerated
by a faithful report of the tranquillity and cheerfulness
of the lady herself, and my love subsided in friendship
and esteem." The probability, indeed, that he and
Mdlle. Curchod would ever see each other again, must
have seemed remote in the extreme. Europe and England
were involved in the Seven Years War ; he was fixed at
home, and an officer in the militia; Switzerland was
far off : when and where were they likely to meet ?

They did, contrary to all expectation, meet again, and
renewed terms not so much of friendship as of affection.
Mdlle. Curchod, as the wife of Necker, became somewhat
of a celebrity, and it is chiefly owing to these last-named
circumstances that the world has ever heard of Gibbon's
early love.

While he was at Lausanne Gibbon made the acquaintance of Voltaire, but it led to no intimacy or fruitful
reminiscence. "He received me with civility as an
English youth, but I cannot boast of any peculiar notice
or distinction." Still he had "the satisfaction of hearing—an uncommon circumstance—a great poet declaim
his own productions on the stage." One is often
tempted, in reading Gibbon's Memoirs, to regret that
he adopted the austere plan which led him "to condemn
the practice of transforming a private memorial into a
vehicle of satire or praise." As he truly says, "It was
assuredly in his power to amuse the reader with a gal-
lery of portraits and a collection of anecdotes." This
reserve is particularly disappointing when a striking
and original figure like Voltaire passes across the field,
without an attempt to add one stroke to the portraiture
of such a physiognomy.

Gibbon had now (1758) been nearly five years at
Lausanne, when his father suddenly intimated that he
was to return home immediately. The Seven Years War
was at its height, and the French had denied a passage
through France to English travellers. Gibbon, or more
properly his Swiss friends, thought that the alternative
road through Germany might be dangerous, though it
might have been assumed that the Great Frederick, so far
as he was concerned, would make things as pleasant as
possible to British subjects, whose country had just

consented to supply him with a much-needed subsidy. The French route was preferred, perhaps as much from a motive of frolic as anything else. Two Swiss officers of his acquaintance undertook to convey Gibbon from France as one of their companions, under an assumed name, and in borrowed regimentals. His complete mastery of French removed any chance of detection on the score of language, and with a "mixture of joy and regret" on the 11th April, 1758, Gibbon left Lausanne. He had a pleasant journey, but no adventures, and returned to his native land after an absence of four years, ten months, and fifteen days.

CHAPTER III.

THE only person whom, on his return, Gibbon had the least wish to see was his aunt, Catherine Porten. To her house he at once hastened, and " the evening was spent in the effusions of joy and tenderness." He looked forward to his first meeting with his father with no slight anxiety, and that for two reasons. First, his father had parted from him with anger and menace, and he had no idea how he would be received now. Secondly, his mother's place was occupied by a second wife, and an involuntary but strong prejudice possessed him against his step-mother. He was most agreeably disappointed in both respects. His father " received him as a man, as a friend, all constraint was banished at our first interview, and we ever after continued on the same terms of easy and equal politeness." So far the prospect was pleasant. But the step-mother remained a possible obstacle to all comfort at home. He seems to have regarded his father's second marriage as an act of displeasure with himself, and he was disposed to hate the rival of his mother. Gibbon soon found that the injustice was in his own fancy, and the imaginary monster was an amiable and deserving woman. " I could not be

D

mistaken in the first view of her understanding ; her
knowledge and the elegant spirit of her conversation,
her polite welcome, and her assiduous care to study and
gratify my wishes announced at least that the surface
would be smooth ; and my suspicions of art and false-
hood were gradually dispelled by the full discovery of
her warm and exquisite sensibility." He became indeed
deeply attached to his step-mother. "After some reserve on my side, our minds associated in confidence
and friendship, and as Mrs. Gibbon had neither children
nor the hopes of children, we more easily adopted the
tender names and genuine characters of mother and
son." A most creditable testimony surely to the worth
and amiability of both of them. The friendship thus
begun continued without break or coolness to the end
of Gibbon's life. Thirty-five years after his first interview with his step-mother, and only a few months
before his own death, when he was old and ailing, and
the least exertion, by reason of his excessive corpulence,
involved pain and trouble, he made a long journey to
Bath for the sole purpose of paying Mrs. Gibbon a
visit. He was very far from being the selfish Epicurean
that has been sometimes represented.

He had brought with him from Lausanne the first
pages of a work which, after much bashfulness and
delay, he at length published in the French language,
under the title of *Essai sur l'Étude de la Littérature*, in
the year 1761, that is two years after its completion.
In one respect this juvenile work of Gibbon has little
merit. The style is at once poor and stilted, and the
general quality of remark eminently commonplace,
where it does not fall into paradox. On the other hand,
it has an interesting and even original side. The main

idea of the little book, so far as it has one, was excellent, and really above the general thought of the age, namely, the vindication of classical literature and history generally from the narrow and singular prejudice which prevailed against them, especially in France. When Gibbon ascribes the design of his first work to a "refinement of vanity, the desire of justifying and praising the object of a favourite pursuit," he does himself less than justice. This first utterance of his historic genius was prompted by an unconscious but deep reaction against that contempt for the past, which was the greatest blot in the speculative movement of the eighteenth century. He resists the temper of his time rather from instinct than reason, and pleads the cause of learning with the hesitation of a man who has not fully seen round his subject, or even mastered his own thoughts upon it. Still there is his protest against the proposal of D'Alembert, who recommended that after a selection of facts had been made at the end of every century the remainder should be delivered to the flames. "Let us preserve them all," he says, "most carefully. A Montesquieu will detect in the most insignificant, relations which the vulgar overlook." He resented the haughty pretensions of the mathematical sciences to universal dominion, with sufficient vigour to have satisfied Auguste Comte. "Physics and mathematics are at present on the throne. They see their sister sciences prostrate before them, chained to their chariot, or at most occupied in adorning their triumph. Perhaps their downfall is not far off." To speak of a positive downfall of exact sciences was a mistake. But we may fairly suppose that Gibbon did not contemplate anything beyond a relative change of

D 2

position in the hierarchy of the sciences, by which
history and politics would recover or attain to a dignity
which was denied them in his day. In one passage
Gibbon shows that he had dimly foreseen the possibility
of the modern inquiries into the conditions of savage
life and prehistoric man. "An Iroquois book, even
were it full of absurdities, would be an invaluable
treasure. It would offer a unique example of the nature
of the human mind placed in circumstances which we
have never known, and influenced by manners and religious opinions, the complete opposite of ours." In
this sentence Gibbon seems to call in anticipation for
the researches which have since been prosecuted with
so much success by eminent writers among ourselves,
not to mention similar inquirers on the Continent.

But in the meantime Gibbon had entered on a career
which removed him for long months from books and
study. Without sufficiently reflecting on what such a
step involved, he had joined the militia, which was em-
bodied in the year 1760 ; and for the next two and a
half years led, as he says, a wandering life of military
servitude. At first, indeed, he was so pleased with
his new mode of life that he had serious thoughts of
becoming a professional soldier. But this enthusiasm
speedily wore off, and our "mimic Bellona soon revealed
to his eyes her naked deformity." It was indeed no
mere playing at soldiering that he had undertaken.
He was the practical working commander of "an independent corps of 476 officers and men." "In the
absence, or even in the presence of the two field
officers" (one of whom was his father, the major) "I
was intrusted with the effective labour of dictating the
orders and exercising the battalion." And his duty did

not consist in occasional drilling and reviews, but in
serious marches, sometimes of thirty miles in a day, and
camping under canvas.   One encampment, on Win-
chester Downs, lasted four months.   Gibbon does not
hesitate to say that the superiority of his grenadiers
to the detachments of the regular army, with which they
were often mingled, was so striking that the most prejudiced regular could not have hesitated a moment to
admit it.   But the drilling, and manœuvring, and all
that pertained to the serious side of militia business
interested Gibbon, and though it took up time it gave
him knowledge of a special kind, of which he quite
appreciated the value.   He was much struck, for
instance, by the difference between the nominal and
effective force of every regiment he had seen, even
when supposed to be complete, and gravely doubts
whether a nominal army of 100,000 men often brings
fifty thousand into the field.   What he found unen-
durable was the constant shifting of quarters, the utter
want of privacy and leisure it often entailed, and the
distasteful society in which he was forced to live.   For
eight months at a stretch he never took a book in his
hand.   "From the day we marched from Blandford, I
had hardly a moment I could call my own, being almost
continually in motion, or if I was fixed for a day, it was
in the guardroom, a barrack, or an inn."   Even worse
were the drinking and late hours ; sometimes in "rustic"
company, sometimes in company in which joviality and
wit were more abundant than decorum and common sense,
which will surprise no one who hears that the famous
John Wilkes, who was colonel of the Buckingham
militia, was not unfrequently one of his boon companions.   A few extracts from his journal will be enough.

"To-day (August 28, 1762), Sir Thomas Worsley," the
colonel of the battalion, "came to us to dinner.
Pleased to see him, we kept bumperising till after
roll-calling, Sir Thomas assuring us every fresh bottle
how infinitely sober he was growing." September 23rd.
"Colonel Wilkes, of the Buckingham militia, dined with
us, and renewed the acquaintance Sir Thomas and
myself had begun with him at Reading. I scarcely
ever met with a better companion; he has inexhaustible spirits, infinite wit and humour, and a great deal
of knowledge . . . This proved a very debauched day;
we drank a great deal both after dinner and supper;
and when at last Wilkes had retired, Sir Thomas and
some others (of whom I was not one) broke into his
room and made him drink a bottle of claret in bed."
December 17. "We found old Captain Meard at
Arlesford with the second division of the Fourteenth.
He and all his officers supped with us, which made the
evening rather a drunken one." Gibbon might well
say that the militia was unfit for and unworthy of him.

Yet it is quite astonishing to see, as recorded in his
journal, how keen an interest he still managed to retain
in literature in the midst of all this dissipation, and
how fertile he was of schemes and projects of future
historical works to be prosecuted under more favourable
auspices. Subject after subject occurred to him as
eligible and attractive; he caresses the idea for a time,
then lays it aside for good reasons. First, he pitched
upon the expedition of Charles VIII. of France into
Italy. He read and meditated upon it, and wrote a
dissertation of ten folio pages, besides large notes, in
which he examined the right of Charles VIII. to the
crown of Naples, and the rival claims of the houses of

Anjou and Aragon. In a few weeks he gives up this idea,
firstly, for the rather odd reason that the subject was too
remote from us; and, secondly, for the very good reason
that the expedition was rather the introduction to great
events than great and important in itself. He then successively chose and rejected the Crusade of Richard the
First; the Barons' War against John and Henry III.; the
history of Edward the Black Prince; the lives and comparisons of Henry V. and the Emperor Titus; the life of
Sir Philip Sidney, and that of the Marquis of Montrose.
At length he fixed on Sir Walter Raleigh as his hero.
On this he worked with all the assiduity that his militia
life allowed, read a great quantity of original documents relating to it, and, after some months of labour,
declared that "his subject opened upon him, and in
general improved upon a nearer prospect." But half a
year later he "is afraid he will have to drop his hero."
And he covers half a page with reasons to persuade
himself that he was right in doing so. Besides the
obvious one that he would be able to add little that
was not already accessible in Oldys' *Life of Raleigh*,
that the topic was exhausted, and so forth, he goes on
to make these remarks, which have more signification to
us now than perhaps they had to him when he wrote
them. "Could I even surmount these obstacles, I
should shrink with terror from the modern history of
England, where every character is a problem and every
reader a friend or an enemy : when a writer is supposed
to hoist a flag of party, and is devoted to damnation by
the adverse faction. Such would be *my* reception at
home ; and abroad the historian of Raleigh must encounter an indifference far more bitter than censure or
reproach. The events of his life are interesting ; but

his character is ambiguous ; his actions are obscure ; his
writings are English, and his fame is confined to the
narrow limits of our language and our island. *I must
embrace a safer and more extensive theme.*" Here we
see the first gropings after a theme of cosmopolitan
interest. He has arrived at two negative conclusions :
that it must not be English, and must not be narrow.
What it is to be, does not yet appear, for he has still a
series of subjects to go through, to be taken up and
discarded. The history of the liberty of the Swiss,
which at a later period he partially achieved, was one
scheme ; the history of Florence under the Medici was
another. He speaks with enthusiasm of both projects,
adding that he will most probably fix upon the latter ;
but he never did anything of the kind.

These were the topics which occupied Gibbon's mind
during his service in the militia, escaping when he could
from the uproar and vulgarity of the camp and the
guardroom to the sanctuary of the historic muse, to
worship in secret. But these private devotions could
not remove his disgust at "the inn, the wine, and the
company " he was forced to endure, and latterly the
militia became downright insupportable to him. But
honourable motives kept him to his post. " From a
service without danger I might have retired without
disgrace ; but as often as I hinted a wish of re-
signing, my fetters were riveted by the friendly intreaties of the colonel, the parental authority of the
major, and my own regard for the welfare of the
battalion." At last the long-wished-for day arrived,
when the militia was disbanded. " Our two com-
panies," he writes in his journal, " were disembodied
(December 23rd, 1762), mine at Alton, my father's at

Buriton. They fired three volleys, lodged the major's colours, delivered up their arms, received their money, partook of a dinner at the major's expense, and then separated, with great cheerfulness and regularity. Thus ended the militia." The compression that his spirit had endured was shown by the rapid energy with which he sought a change of scene and oblivion of his woes. Within little more than a month after the scene just described, Gibbon was in Paris beginning the grand tour.

With that keen sense of the value of time which marked him, Gibbon with great impartiality cast up and estimated the profit and loss of his "bloodless campaigns." Both have been alluded to already. He summed up with great fairness in the entry that he made in his journal on the evening of the day on which he recovered his liberty. "I am glad that the militia has been, and glad that it is no more." This judgment he confirmed thirty years afterwards, when he composed his Memoirs. "My principal obligation to the militia was the making me an Englishman and a soldier. After my foreign education, with my reserved temper, I should long have continued a stranger in my native country, had I not been shaken in this various scene of new faces and new friends; had not experience forced me to feel the characters of our leading men, the state of parties, the forms of office, the operations of our civil and military system. In this peaceful service I imbibed the rudiments of the language and science of tactics, which opened a new field of study and observation. I diligently read and meditated the *Mémoires Militaires* of Quintus Icilius, the only writer who has united the merits of a professor and a veteran.

The discipline and evolution of a modern battalion gave
me a clearer notion of the phalanx and the legion, and
the captain of the Hampshire grenadiers (the reader
may smile) has not been useless to the historian of the
Roman Empire." No one can doubt it who compares
Gibbon's numerous narratives of military operations
with the ordinary performances of civil historians in
those matters. The campaigns of Julian, Belisarius,
and Heraclius, not to mention many others, have not
only an uncommon lucidity, but also exhibit a clear
appreciation of the obstacles and arduousness of war-
like operations, which is rare or unknown to non-
military writers. Macaulay has pointed out that
Swift's party pamphlets are superior in an especial
way to the ordinary productions of that class, in
consequence of Swift's unavowed but very serious
participation in the cabinet councils of Oxford and
Bolingbroke. In the same manner Gibbon had an
advantage through his military training, which gives
him no small superiority to even the best historical
writers who have been without it.

The course of foreign travel which Gibbon was now
about to commence had been contemplated before, but
the war and the militia had postponed it for nearly
three years. It appears that as early as the year 1760
the elder Gibbon had conceived the project of procuring
a seat in Parliament for his son, and was willing to
incur the anticipated expense of £1500 for that object.
Young Gibbon, who seems to have very accurately gauged
his own abilities at that early age, was convinced that
the money could be much better employed in another
way. He wrote in consequence, under his father's roof,
a letter to the latter which does such credit to his

head and to his heart, that, although it is somewhat
long, it cannot with propriety be omitted here.

EDWARD GIBBON TO HIS FATHER.

"DEAR SIR,

"An address in writing from a person who has the
pleasure of being with you every day may appear singular.
However I have preferred this method, as upon paper I can
speak without a blush and be heard without interruption.
If my letter displeases you, impute it, dear sir, to yourself.
You have treated me, not like a son, but like a friend. Can
you be surprised that I should communicate to a friend all
my thoughts and all my desires? Unless the friend approve
them, let the father never know them; or at least let him
know at the same time that however reasonable, however
eligible, my scheme may appear to me, I would rather forget
it for ever than cause him the slightest uneasiness.

"When I first returned to England, attentive to my future
interests, you were so good as to give me hopes of a seat in
Parliament. This seat, it was supposed, would be an expense
of fifteen hundred pounds. This design flattered my vanity,
as it might enable me to shine in so august an assembly. It
flattered a nobler passion: I promised myself that, by the
means of this seat, I might one day be the instrument of some
good to my country. But I soon perceived how little mere
virtuous inclination, unassisted by talents, could contribute
towards that great end, and a very short examination discovered
to me that those talents had not fallen to my lot. Do not,
dear sir, impute this declaration to a false modesty—the meanest
species of pride. Whatever else I may be ignorant of, I think I
know myself, and shall always endeavour to mention my good
qualities without vanity and my defects without repugnance.
I shall say nothing of the most intimate acquaintance with his
country and language, so absolutely necessary to every senator;
since they may be acquired, to allege my deficiency in them
would seem only the plea of laziness. But I shall say with

great truth that I never possessed that gift of speech, the first
requisite of an orator, which use and labour may improve, but
which nature can alone bestow ; that my temper, quiet, retired,
somewhat reserved, could neither acquire popularity, bear up
against opposition, nor mix with ease in the crowds of public
life ; that even my genius (if you allow me any) is better
qualified for the deliberate compositions of the closet than for
the extempore discourses of Parliament. An unexpected
objection would disconcert me, and as I am incapable of explaining to others what I do not understand myself, I should
be meditating when I ought to be answering. I even want
necessary prejudices of party and of nation. In popular
assemblies it is often necessary to inspire them, and never orator
inspired well a passion which he did not feel himself. Suppose
me even mistaken in my own character, to set out with the
repugnance such an opinion must produce offers but an in-
different prospect. But I hear you say it is not necessary that
every man should enter into Parliament with such exalted
hopes. It is to acquire a title the most glorious of any in a
free country, and to employ the weight and consideration it
gives in the service of one's friends. Such motives, though not
glorious, yet are not dishonourable, and if we had a borough in
our command, if you could bring me in without any great
expense, or if our fortune enabled us to despise that expense,
then indeed I should think them of the greatest strength. But
with our private fortune, is it worth while to purchase at so high
a rate a title honourable in itself, but which I must share with
every fellow that can lay out 1500 pounds ? Besides, dear
sir, a merchandise is of little value to the owner when he is
resolved not to sell it.

" I should affront your penetration did I not suppose you now
see the drift of this letter. It is to appropriate to another use
the sum with which you destined to bring me into Parliament ;
to employ it, not in making me great, but in rendering me
happy. I have often heard you say yourself that the allowance
you had been so indulgent as to grant me, though very liberal
in regard to your estate, was yet but small when compared with
the almost necessary extravagances of the age. I have indeed

found it so, notwithstanding a good deal of economy, and an exemption from many of the common expenses of youth. This, dear sir, would be a way of supplying these deficiencies without any additional expense to you. But I forbear—if you think my proposals reasonable, you want no intreaties to engage you to comply with them, if otherwise all will be without effect.

"All that I am afraid of, dear sir, is that I should seem not so much asking a favour, as this really is, as exacting a debt. After all I can say, you will remain the best judge of my good and your own circumstances. Perhaps, like most landed gentlemen, an addition to my annuity would suit you better than a sum of money given at once ; perhaps the sum itself may be too considerable. Whatever you may think proper to bestow on me, or in whatever manner, will be received with equal gratitude.

"I intended to stop here, but as I abhor the least appearance of art, I think it better to lay open my whole scheme at once. The unhappy war which now desolates Europe will oblige me to defer seeing France till a peace. But that reason can have no influence on Italy, a country which every scholar must long to see. Should you grant my request, and not disapprove of my manner of employing your bounty, I would leave England this autumn and pass the winter at Lausanne with M. de Voltaire and my old friends. In the spring I would cross the Alps, and after some stay in Italy, as the war must then be terminated, return home through France, to live happily with you and my dear mother. I am now two-and-twenty ; a tour must take up a considerable time; and although I believe you have no thoughts of settling me soon (and I am sure I have not), yet so many things may intervene that the man who does not travel early runs a great risk of not travelling at all. But this part of my scheme, as well as the whole of it, I submit entirely to you.

"Permit me, dear sir, to add that I do not know whether the complete compliance with my wishes could increase my love and gratitude, but that I am very sure no refusal could diminish those sentiments with which I shall always remain, dear sir, your most dutiful and obedient son and servant.

"E. GIBBON, Jun."

Instead of going to Italy in the autumn of 1760, as he fondly hoped when he wrote this letter, Gibbon was marching about the south of England at the head of his grenadiers.   But the scheme sketched in the above letter was only postponed, and ultimately realised in every particular   The question of a seat in Parliament never came up again during his father's life, and no doubt the money it would have cost was, according to his wise suggestion, devoted to defray the expenses of his foreign tour, which he is now about to begin.

CHAPTER IV.

GIBBON reached Paris on the 28th January, 1763;
thirty-six days, as he tells us, after the disbanding of
the militia. He remained a little over three months in
the French capital, which on the whole pleased him
so well that he thinks that if he had been independent
and rich, he might have been tempted to make it his
permanent residence.

On the other hand he seems to have been little if at
all aware of the extraordinary character of the society
of which he became a spectator and for a time a member.
He does not seem to have been conscious that he was
witnessing one of the most singular social phases which
have yet been presented in the history of man. And
no blame attaches to him for this. No one of his contemporaries saw deeper in this direction than he did.
It is a remarkable instance of the way in which the
widest and deepest social movements are veiled to the
eyes of those who see them, precisely because of their
width and depth. Foreigners, especially Englishmen,
visited Paris in the latter half of the eighteenth century
and reported variously of their experience and impressions. Some, like Hume and Sterne, are delighted;

some, like Gibbon, are quietly, but thoroughly pleased;
some, like Walpole—though he perhaps is a class by
himself—are half pleased and half disgusted. They
all feel that there is something peculiar in what they
witness, but never seem to suspect that nothing like it
was ever seen before in the world. One is tempted to
wish that they could have seen with our eyes, or, much
more, that we could have had the privilege of enjoying
their experience, of spending a few months in that
singular epoch when "society," properly so called, the
assembling of men and women in drawing-rooms for
the purpose of conversation, was the most serious as
well as the most delightful business of life. Talk and
discussion in the senate, the market-place, and the
schools are cheap; even barbarians are not wholly
without them. But their refinement and concentration
in the *salon*—of which the president is a woman of tact
and culture—this is a phenomenon which never appeared
but in Paris in the eighteenth century. And yet scholars,
men of the world, men of business passed through this
wonderland with eyes blindfolded. They are free to
enter, they go, they come, without a sign that they have
realised the marvellous scene that they were permitted
to traverse. One does not wonder that they did not
perceive that in those graceful drawing-rooms, filled
with stately company of elaborate manners, ideas and
sentiments were discussed and evolved which would
soon be more explosive than gunpowder. One does
not wonder that they did not see ahead of them—men
never do. One does rather wonder that they did not
see what was before their eyes. But wonder is useless
and a mistake. People who have never seen a volcano

cannot be expected to fear the burning lava, or even to
see that a volcano differs from any other mountain.

   Gibbon had brought good introductions from London,
but he admits that they were useless, or rather superfluous.   His nationality and his *Essai* were his best
recommendations.   It was the day of Anglomania, and,
as he says, "every Englishman was supposed to be a
patriot and a philosopher."   "I had rather be," said
Mdlle. de Lespinasse to Lord Shelburne, "the least
member of the House of Commons than even the King
of Prussia."   Similar things must have been said to
Gibbon, but he has not recorded them; and generally
it may be said that he is disappointingly dull and in-
different to Paris, though he liked it well enough when
there.   He never caught the Paris fever as Hume did, and
Sterne, or even as Walpole did, for all the hard things he
says of the underbred and overbearing manners of the
philosophers.   Gibbon had ready access to the well-known
houses of Madame Geoffrin, Madame Helvétius and
the Baron d'Holbach; and his perfect mastery of the
language must have removed every obstacle in the way
of complete social intercourse.   But no word in his
Memoirs or Letters shows that he really saw with the
eyes of the mind the singularities of that strange
epoch.   And yet he was there at an exciting and important moment.   The Order of the Jesuits was tottering
to its fall; the latter volumes of the *Encyclopedia* were
being printed, and it was no secret; the coruscating
wit and audacity of the *salons* were at their height.
He is not unjust or prejudiced, but somewhat cold.
He dines with Baron d'Holbach, and says his dinners
were excellent, but nothing of the guests.   He goes to
Madame Geoffrin, and pronounces her house an excellent

E

one. Such faint and commonplace praise reflects on the eulogist. The only man of letters of whom he speaks with warmth is Helvétius. He does not appear in this first visit to have known Madame du Deffand, who was still keeping her *salon* with the help of the pale deep-eyed L'Espinasse, though the final rupture was imminent. Louis Racine died, and so did Marivaux, while he was in Paris. The old Opera-house in the Palais Royal was burnt down when he had been there a little over a month, and the representations were transferred to the Salle des Machines, in the Tuileries. The equestrian statue of Louis XV. was set up in the Place to which it gave its name (where the Luxor column now stands, in the Place de la Concorde) amidst the jeers and insults of the mob, who declared it would never be got to pass the hotel of Madame de Pompadour. How much or how little of all this touched Gibbon, we do not know. We do know one thing, that his English clothes were unfashionable and looked very foreign, the French being "excessively long-waisted." Doubtless his scanty purse could not afford a new outfit, such as Walpole two years afterwards, under the direction of Lady Hertford, promptly procured. On the 8th of May he hurried off to Lausanne.[1]

His ultimate object was Italy. But he wisely resolved to place a period of solid study between the lively dissipation of Paris and his classic pilgrimage. He knew the difference between seeing things he had read about and reading about things after he had seen them; how the mind, charged with associations of famous scenes, is delicately susceptible of impressions, and how

[1] The chronicle of events which occurred during Gibbon's sojourn in Paris will be found in the interesting *Mémoires de Bachaumont.*

rapidly old musings take form and colour, when
stirred by outward realities ; and contrariwise, how slow
and inadequate is the effort to reverse this process, and
to clothe with memories, monuments and sites over
which the spirit has not sent a halo of previous meditation. So he settled down quietly at Lausanne for the
space of nearly a year, and commenced a most austere
and systematic course of reading on the antiquities of
Italy. The list of learned works which he perused
" with his pen in his hand " is formidable, and fills a
quarto page. But he went further than this, and com-
piled an elaborate treatise on the nations, provinces, and
towns of ancient Italy (which we still have) digested in
alphabetical order, in which every Latin author, from
Plautus to Rutilius, is laid under contribution for
illustrative passages, which are all copied out in full.
This laborious work was evidently Gibbon's own guide-
book in his Italian travels, and one sees not only
what an admirable preparation it was for the object in
view, but what a promise it contained of that scrupulous
thoroughness which was to be his mark as an historian.
His mind was indeed rapidly maturing, and becoming
conscious in what direction its strength lay.

His account of his first impressions of Rome has
been often quoted, and deserves to be so again. " My
temper is not very susceptible of enthusiasm, and the
enthusiasm which I do not feel I have ever scorned to
affect. But at the distance of twenty-five years I can
neither forget nor express the strong emotions which
agitated my mind as I first approached and entered the
Eternal City. After a sleepless night, I trod with a
lofty step the ruins of the Forum. Each memorable spot
where Romulus stood, or Tully spoke, or Cæsar fell, was

at once present to my eye, and several days of intoxication were lost and enjoyed before I could descend to a
cool and minute examination." He gave eighteen weeks to
the study of Rome only, and six to Naples, and we may
rest assured that he made good use of his time. But
what makes this visit to Rome memorable in his life
and in literary history is that it was the occasion and
date of the first conception of his great work. "It was
at Rome, on the 15th October, 1764, as I sat musing
amid the ruins of the Capitol, while the barefooted
friars were singing vespers in the temple of Jupiter,
that the idea of writing the decline and fall of the city
first started to my mind." The scene, the contrast of
the old religion and the new, the priests of Christ
replacing the flamens of Jupiter, the evensong of
Catholic Rome swelling like a dirge over the prostrate
Pagan Rome might well concentrate in one grand
luminous idea the manifold but unconnected thoughts
with which his mind had so long been teeming. Gibbon
had found his work, which was destined to fill the
remainder of his life. Henceforth there is a fixed
centre around which his thoughts and musings cluster
spontaneously. Difficulties and interruptions are not
wanting. The plan then formed is not taken in hand
at once ; on the contrary, it is contemplated at "an awful
distance" ; but it led him on like a star guiding his
steps, till he reached his appointed goal.

After crossing the Alps on his homeward journey,
Gibbon had had some thoughts of visiting the southern
provinces of France. But when he reached Lyons he
found letters "expressive of some impatience" for his
return. Though he does not exactly say as much, we
may justly conclude that the elder Gibbon's pecuniary

difficulties were beginning to be oppressive. So the traveller, with the dutifulness that he ever showed to his father, at once bent his steps northward. Again he passed through Paris, and the place had a new attraction in his eyes in the person of Mdlle. Curchod, now become Madame Necker, and wife of the great financier.

This perhaps will be the most convenient place to notice and estimate a certain amount of rather spiteful gossip, of which Gibbon was the subject in Switzerland about this time. Rousseau and his friend Moultou have preserved it for us, and it is probable that it has lost none of its pungency in passing through the hands of the latter. The substance of it is this:—that in the year 1763, when Gibbon revisited Lausanne, as we have seen, Susanne Curchod was still in a pitiable state of melancholy and well nigh broken-hearted at Gibbon's manifest coldness, which we know he considered to be "friendship and esteem." Whether he even saw her on this visit cannot be considered certain, but it is at least highly probable. Be that as it may : this is the picture of her condition as drawn by Moultou in a letter to Rousseau : "How sorry I am for our poor Mdlle. Curchod! Gibbon, whom she loves, and to whom I know she has sacrificed some excellent matches, has come to Lausanne, but cold, insensible, and as entirely cured of his old passion as she is far from cure. She has written me a letter that makes my heart ache." Rousseau says in reply, "He who does not appreciate Mdlle. Curchod is not worthy of her ; he who appreciates her and separates himself from her is a man to be despised. She does not know what she wants. Gibbon serves her better than her own heart. I would rather a hundred times that he left her poor and free among you than

that he should take her off to be rich and miserable in
England." One does not quite see how Gibbon could
have acted to the contentment of Jean-Jacques. For
not taking Mdlle. Curchod to England—as we may presume he would have done if he had married her—he
is contemptible. Yet if he does take her he will
make her miserable, and Rousseau would rather a
hundred times he left her alone—precisely what he was
doing ; but then he was despicable for doing it. The
question is whether there is not a good deal of exaggeration in all this. Only a year after the tragic condition
in which Moultou describes Mdlle. Curchod she married
M. Necker, and became devoted to her husband. A few
months after she married Necker she cordially invited
Gibbon to her house every day of his sojourn in
Paris. If Gibbon had behaved in the unworthy way
asserted, if she had had her feelings so profoundly
touched and lacerated as Moultou declares, would she, or
even could she, have acted thus ? If she was conscious
of being wronged, and he was conscious—as he must have
been—of having acted basely, or at least unfeelingly, is
it not as good as certain that both parties would have
been careful to see as little of each other as possible ?
A broken-off love-match, even without complication of
unworthy conduct on either side, is generally an effective
bar to further intercourse. But in this case the intercourse is renewed on the very first opportunity, and
never dropped till the death of one of the persons
concerned.

Two letters have been preserved of Gibbon and
Madame Necker respectively, nearly of the same date,
and both referring to this rather delicate topic of their
first interviews after her marriage. Gibbon writes to

his friend Holroyd, "The Curchod (Madame Necker)
I saw in Paris. She was very fond of me, and the
husband particularly civil. Could they insult me more
cruelly? Ask me every evening to supper, go to bed
and leave me alone with his wife—what impertinent
security! It is making an old lover of mighty little
consequence. She is as handsome as ever, and much
genteeler; seems pleased with her wealth rather than
proud of it. I was exalting Nanette d'Illens's good luck
and the fortune " (this evidently refers to some common
acquaintance, who had changed her name to advantage).
" 'What fortune,' she said with an air of contempt :—
'not above twenty thousand livres a year.' I smiled,
and she caught herself immediately, 'What airs I
give myself in despising twenty thousand livres a year,
who a year ago looked upon eight hundred as the summit
of my wishes.' "

Let us turn to the lady's account of the same
scenes. "I do not know if I told you," she writes to
a friend at Lausanne, "that I have seen Gibbon, and it
has given me more pleasure than I know how to express.
Not indeed that I retain any sentiment for a man who
I think does not deserve much " (this little toss of
pique or pride need not mislead us) ; " but my feminine
vanity could not have had a more complete and honest
triumph. He stayed two weeks in Paris, and I had him
every day at my house ; he has become soft, yielding,
humble, decorous to a fault. He was a constant witness
of my husband's kindness, wit, and gaiety, and made
me remark for the first time, by his admiration for
wealth, the opulence with which I am surrounded, and
which up to this moment had only produced a dis-
agreeable impression upon me." Considering the very

different points of view of the writers, these letters are
remarkably in unison. The solid fact of the daily visits
is recorded in both. It is easy to gather from Madame
Necker's letter that she was very glad to show Mr.
Gibbon that for going farther and not marrying him
she had not fared worse. The rather acid allusion to
" opulence " is found in both letters; but much more
pronounced in hers than in his. Each hints that the
other thought too much of wealth. But he does so with
delicacy, and only by implication; she charges him
coarsely with vulgar admiration for it. We may reasonably suspect that riches had been the subject of not
altogether smooth conversation between them, in the later
part of the evening, perhaps, after M. Necker had retired
in triumph to bed. One might even fancy that there
was a tacit allusion by Madame Necker to the dialogue
recorded by Gibbon to Holroyd, when his smile checked
her indirect pride in her own wealth, and that she
remembered that smile with just a touch of resentment.
If so, nothing was more natural and comforting than to
charge him with the failing that he had detected in her.
But here are the facts. Eight months after her marriage, Madame Necker admits that she had Gibbon every
day to her house. He says that she was very cordial.
She would have it understood that she received him only
for the sake of gratifying a feminine vanity. For her
own sake one might prefer his interpretation to hers.
It is difficult to believe that the essentially simple-
minded Madame Necker would have asked a man every
day to her house merely to triumph over him; and
more difficult still to believe that the man would have
gone if such had been the object. A little tartness in
these first interviews, following on a relation of some

ambiguity, cannot surprise one. But it was not the
dominant ingredient, or the interviews must have ceased
of their own accord. In any case few will admit that
either of the persons concerned would have written as
they did if Moultou's statement were correct. In
neither epistle is there any trace of a grand passion
felt or slighted. We discover the much lower level
of vanity and badinage. And the subsequent relations
of Gibbon and Madame Necker all tend to prove that
this was the real one.

CHAPTER V.

GIBBON now (June, 1765) returned to his father's house,
and remained there till the latter's death in 1770. He
describes these five years as having been the least
pleasant and satisfactory of his whole life. The reasons
were not far to seek. The unthrifty habits of the elder
Gibbon were now producing their natural result. He
was saddled with debt, from which two mortgages,
readily consented to by his son, and the sale of the
house at Putney, only partially relieved him. Gibbon
now began to fear that he had an old age of poverty
before him. He had pursued knowledge with single-
hearted loyalty and now became aware that from a
worldly point of view knowledge is not often a profitable
investment. A more dejecting discovery cannot be made
by the sincere scholar. He is conscious of labour and
protracted effort, which the prosperous professional
man and tradesman who pass him on their road to
wealth with a smile of scornful pity have never known.
He has forsaken comparatively all for knowledge, and
the busy world meets him with a blank stare, and surmises
shrewdly that he is but an idler, with an odd taste for

wasting his time over books. It says much for
Gibbon's robustness of spirit that he did not break
down in these trying years, that he did not weakly take
fright at his prospect, and make hasty and violent efforts
to mend it. On the contrary, he remained steadfast and
true to the things of the mind. With diminished cheerfulness perhaps, but with no abatement of zeal, he pursued his course and his studies, thereby proving that he
belonged to the select class of the strong and worthy
who, penetrated with the loveliness of science, will not
be turned away from it.

His first effort to redeem the time was a project of
a history of Switzerland. His choice was decided by
two circumstances : (1) his love for a country which he
had made his own by adoption ; (2) by the fact that he
had in his friend Deyverdun, a fellow-worker who could
render him most valuable assistance. Gibbon never
knew German, which is not surprising when we reflect
what German literature amounted to, in those days ;
and he soon discovered that the most valuable authorities of his projected work were in the German
language. But Deyverdun was a perfect master of
that tongue, and translated a mass of documents for
the use of his friend. They laboured for two years
in collecting materials, before Gibbon felt himself
justified in entering on the " more agreeable task of
composition." And even then he considered the preparation insufficient, as no doubt it was. He felt he
could not do justice to his subject ; uninformed as he
was " by the scholars and statesmen, and remote from
the archives and libraries of the Swiss republic." Such
a beginning was not of good augury for the success of
the undertaking. He never wrote more than about

sixty quarto pages of the projected work, and these, as
they were in French, were submitted to the judgment of
a literary society of foreigners in London, before whom
the MS. was read.   The author was unknown, and
Gibbon attended the meeting, and thus listened without
being observed " to the free strictures and unfavourable
sentence of his judges."   He admits that the momentary
sensation was painful; but the condemnation was
ratified by his cooler thoughts : and he declares that he
did not regret the loss of a slight and superficial essay,
though it "had cost some expense, much labour, and
more time."   He says in his Memoirs that he burnt the
sheets.   But this, strange to say, was a mistake on his
part.   They were found among his papers after his
death, and though not published by Lord Sheffield in
the first two volumes of his Miscellaneous Works, which
the latter edited in 1796, they appeared in the supple-
mental third volume which came out in 1815. We thus
can judge for ourselves of their value.   One sees at
once why and how they failed to satisfy their author's
mature judgment.   They belong to that style of historical writing which consists in the rhetorical transcription
and adornment of the original authorities, but in which
the writer never gets close enough to his subject to
apply the touchstone of a clear and trenchant criticism.
Such criticism indeed was not common in Switzerland
in his day, and one cannot blame Gibbon for not antici-
pating the researches of modern investigators.   But his
historical sense was aroused to suspicion by the story of
William Tell, which he boldly sets down as a fable.
Altogether, one may pronounce the sketch to be pleasantly
written in a flowing, picturesque narrative, and showing
immense advance in style beyond the essay on the Study

of Literature. David Hume, to whom he submitted it, urged him to persevere, and the advice was justified under the circumstances, although one cannot now regret that it was not followed.

After the failure of this scheme Gibbon, still in connection with Deyverdun, planned a periodical work under the title of *Mémoires Littéraires de la Grande Bretagne.* Only two volumes ever appeared, and the speculation does not seem to have met with much success. Gibbon " presumes to say that their merit was superior to their reputation, though they produced more reputation than emolument." The first volume is executed with evident pains, and gives a fair picture of the literary and social condition of England at the time. The heavy review articles are interspersed with what is intended to be lighter matter on the fashions, foibles, and prominent characters of the day. Gibbon owns the authorship of the first article on Lord Lyttelton's history of Henry the Second, and his hand is discernible in the account of the fourth volume of Lardner's work *On the Credibility of the Gospel History.* The first has no merit beyond a faithful report. The latter is written with much more zest and vigour, and shows the interest that he already took in Christian antiquities. Other articles, evidently from the pen of Deyverdun, on the English theatre and Beau Nash of Bath, are the liveliest in the collection. The magazine was avowedly intended for Continental readers, and might have obtained success if it had been continued long enough. But it died before it had time to make itself known.[1]

[1] Two volumes appeared of the *Mémoires Littéraires.* Of these only the first is to be found in the British Museum. It is a small 12mo, containing 230 pages. Here is the Table des Matières :—(1)

When the *Mémoires Littéraires* collapsed Gibbon was
again left without a definite object to concentrate his
energy, and with his work still to seek. One might
wonder why he did not seriously prepare for the *Decline
and Fall*. It must have been chiefly at this time that
it was "contemplated at an awful distance," perhaps
even with numbing doubt whether the distance would
ever be lessened and the work achieved, or even begun.
The probability is he had too little peace of mind to
undertake anything that required calm and protracted
labour. "While so many of my acquaintance were
married, or in Parliament, or advancing with a rapid
step in the various roads of honour or fortune I stood
alone, immovable, and insignificant. . . . The progress
and the knowledge of our domestic disorders aggravated
my anxiety, and I began to apprehend that in my old
age I might be left without the fruits of either industry
or inheritance." Perhaps a reasonable apprehension of
poverty is more paralysing than the reality. In the
latter case prompt action is so imperatively commanded
that the mind has no leisure for the fatal indulgence of
regrets; but when indigence seems only imminent, and
has not yet arrived, a certain lethargy is apt to be produced out of which only the most practical characters can
rouse themselves, and these are not, as a rule, scholars
by nature. We need not be surprised that Gibbon

Histoire de Henri II., par Milord Lyttelton; (2) Le Nouveau
Guide de Bath; (3) Essai sur l'Histoire de la Société Civile, par
M. Ferguson; (4) Conclusions des Mémoires de Miss Sydney
Bidulph; Théologie (5) Recueil des Témoignages Anciens, par
Lardner; (6) Le Confessional; (7) Transactions Philosophiques;
(8) Le Gouverneur, par D. L. F. Spectacles, Beaux Arts, Nouvelles
Littéraires.

during these years did nothing serious, and postponed undertaking his great work. The inspiration needed to accomplish such a long and arduous course as it implied could not be kindled in a mind harassed by pecuniary cares. The fervent heat of a poet's imagination may glow as brightly in poverty as in opulence, but the gentle yet prolonged enthusiasm of the historian is likely to be quenched when the resources of life are too insecure.[1]

It is perhaps not wholly fanciful to suspect that Gibbon's next literary effort was suggested and determined by the inward discomposure he felt at this time. By nature he was not a controversialist; not that he wanted the abilities to support that character, but his mind was too full, fertile, and fond of real knowledge to take much pleasure in the generally barren occupation of gainsaying other men. But at this point in his life he made an exception, and an unprovoked exception. When he wrote his famous vindication of the first volume of the *Decline and Fall* he was acting in self-defence, and repelling savage attacks upon his historical veracity. But in his *Critical Observations on the Sixth Book of the Æneid* he sought controversy for its own sake, and became a polemic—shall we say out of gaiety or bitterness of heart? That inward unrest easily produces an aggressive spirit is a matter of common observation, and it may well have been that in attacking Warburton he sought a diversion from the worry of domestic cares. Be that as it may, his *Obser-*

---

[1] Scholarship has been frequently cultivated amidst great poverty: but from the time of Thucydides, the owner of mines, to Grote, the banker, historians seem to have been in, at least, easy circumstances.

vations are the most pungent and dashing effusion he
ever allowed himself.   It was his first effort in English
prose, and it is doubtful whether he ever managed his
mother tongue better, if indeed he ever managed it so
well.   The little tract is written with singular spirit
and rapidity of style.   It is clear, trenchant, and direct
to a fault.   It is indeed far less critical than polemical,
and shows no trace of lofty calm, either moral or intellectual.   We are not repelled much by his eagerness
to refute and maltreat his opponent.   That was not
alien from the usages of the time, and Warburton at
least had no right to complain of such a style of controversy.   But there is no width and elevation of view.
The writer does not carry the discussion up to a higher
level, and dominate his adversary from a superior standpoint.   Controversy is always ephemeral and vulgar, unless it can rise to the discussion and establishment of
facts and principles valuable for themselves, independently of the particular point at issue.   It is this quality
which has made the master-works of Chillingworth
and Bentley supereminent.   The particular point for
which the writers contended is settled or forgotten.
But in moving up to that point they touched—such was
their large discourse of reason—on topics of perennial
interest, did such justice, though only in passing, to
certain other truths, that they are gratefully remembered
ever after.   Thus Bentley's dissertation on Phalaris is
read, not for the main thesis—proof of the spuriousness
of the letters—but for the profound knowledge and admirable logic with which subsidiary positions are maintained on the way to it.   Tried by this standard, and he
deserves to be tried by a high standard, Gibbon fails
not much, but entirely.   The *Observations* are rarely,

if ever, quoted as an authority of weight by any one
engaged on classical or Virgilian literature. This arises
from the attitude of the writer, who is nearly solely
occupied with establishing negative conclusions that
Æneas was *not* a lawgiver, that the Sixth Æneid is *not*
an allegory, that Virgil had *not* been initiated in the
Eleusinian mysteries when he wrote it, and so forth.
Indeed the best judges now hold that he has not done
full justice to the grain of truth that was to be found
in Warburton's clumsy and prolix hypothesis.[1] It
should be added that Gibbon very candidly admits and
regrets the acrimonious style of the pamphlet, and con-
demns still more "in a personal attack his cowardly
concealment of his name and character."

The *Observations* were the last work which Gibbon
published in his father's lifetime. His account of the
latter's death (November 10, 1770) is feelingly written,
and shows the affectionate side of his own nature to
advantage. He acknowledges his father's failings, his
weakness and inconstancy, but insists that they were
compensated by the virtues of the head and heart, and
the warmest sentiments of honour and humanity. "His
graceful person, polite address, gentle manners, and un-
affected cheerfulness recommended him to the favour
of every company." And Gibbon recalls with emotion
"the pangs of shame, tenderness, and self-reproach"

---

[1] Conington, *Introduction to the Sixth Æneid.* "A reader of the
present day will, I think, be induced to award the palm of learning
and ingenuity to Warburton." "The language and imagery of the
sixth book more than once suggest that Virgil intended to embody
in his picture the poetical view of that inner side of ancient religion
which the mysteries may be supposed to have presented."—*Suggestion on the Study of the Æneid*, by H. Nettleship, p. 13.

which preyed on his father's mind at the prospect, no
doubt, of leaving an embarrassed estate and precarious
fortune to his son and widow. He had no taste for study
in the fatal summer of 1770, and declares that he would
have been ashamed if he had. "I submitted to the
order of nature," he says, in words which recall his
resignation on losing his mistress—"I submitted to the
order of nature, and my grief was soothed by the conscious satisfaction that I had discharged all the duties
of filial piety." We see Gibbon very fairly in this
remark. He had tenderness, steady and warm attach-
ments, but no passion.

Nearly two years elapsed after his father's death,
before he was able to secure from the wreck of his
estate a sufficient competence to establish himself in
London. His house was No. 7, Bentinck Street, near
Manchester Square, then a remote suburb close to the
country fields. His housekeeping was that of a solitary
bachelor, who could afford an occasional dinner-party.
Though not absolutely straitened in means, we shall presently see that he was never quite at his ease in money
matters while he remained in London. But he had now
freedom and no great anxieties, and he began seriously
to contemplate the execution of his great work.

Gibbon, as we have seen, looked back with little satisfaction on the five years between his return from his
travels and his father's death. They are also the years
during which his biographer is able to follow him with
the least certainty. Hardly any of his letters which
refer to that period have been preserved, and he has
glided rapidly over it in his Memoirs. Yet it was, in
other respects besides the matter of pecuniary troubles,
a momentous epoch in his life. The peculiar views

which he adopted and partly professed on religion must
have been formed then. But the date, the circumstance,
and the occasion are left in darkness. Up to December
18, 1763, Gibbon was evidently a believer. In an entry
in his private journal under that date he speaks of a Communion Sunday at Lausanne as affording an "edifying
spectacle," on the ground that there is "neither business
nor parties, and they interdict even whist" on that day.
How soon after this his opinions began to change, it is
impossible to say. But we are conscious of a markedly
different tone in the *Observations*, and a sneer at "the
ancient alliance between the avarice of the priests and
the credulity of the people" is in the familiar style of
the Deists from Toland to Chubb. There is no evidence
of his familiarity with the widely diffused works of the
freethinkers, and as far as I am aware he does not
quote or refer to them even once. But they could hardly
have escaped his notice. Still his strong historic sense
and solid erudition would be more likely to be repelled
than attracted by their vague and inaccurate scholarship, and chimerical theories of the light of Nature.
Still we know that he practically adopted, in the end,
at least the negative portion of these views, and the
question is, When did he do so? His visit to Paris,
and the company that he frequented there, might suggest
that as a probable date of his change of opinions. But
the entry just referred to was subsequent by several
months to that visit, and we may with confidence assume
that no freethinker of the eighteenth century would
pronounce the austerities of a Communion Sunday in
a Calvinist town an edifying spectacle. It is probable
that his relinquishing of dogmatic faith was gradual,
and for a time unconscious. It was an age of tepid

belief, except among the Nonjurors and Methodists ; and
with neither of these groups could he have had the least
sympathy. His acquaintance with Hume, and his partiality for the writings of Bayle, are more probable
sources of a change of sentiment which was in a way
predestined by natural bias and cast of mind. Any
occasion would serve to precipitate the result. In any
case, this result had been attained some years before the
publication of the first volume of the *Decline and Fall*,
in 1776. Referring to his preparatory studies for the
execution of that work, he says, "As I believed, and as
I still believe, that the propagation of the Gospel and
the triumph of the Church are inseparably connected
with the decline of the Roman monarchy, I weighed the
causes and effects of the revolution, and contrasted the
narratives and apologies of the Christians themselves
with the glances of candour or enmity which the pagans
have cast on the rising sects. The Jewish and heathen
testimonies, as they are collected and illustrated by Dr.
Lardner, directed without superseding my search of the
originals, and in an ample dissertation on the miraculous
darkness of the Passion I privately drew my conclusions
from the silence of an unbelieving age." Here we have
the argument which concludes the sixteenth chapter
distinctly announced. But the previous travail of spirit
is not indicated. Gibbon has marked with precision the
stages of his conversion to Romanism. But the following chapters of the history of his religious opinions he
has not written, or he has suppressed them, and we can
only vaguely guess their outline.

CHAPTER VI.

GIBBON's settlement in London as master in his own
house did not come too soon. A few more years of
anxiety and dependence, such as he had passed of late
with his father in the country, would probably have
dried up the spring of literary ambition and made him
miss his career. He had no tastes to fit him for a
country life. The pursuit of farming only pleased him
in Virgil's *Georgics*. He seems neither to have liked
nor to have needed exercise, and English rural sports
had no charms for him. "I never handled a gun, I
seldom mounted a horse, and my philosophic walks
were soon terminated by a shady bench, where I was
long detained by the sedentary amusement of reading
or meditation." He was a born *citadin*. "Never," he
writes to his friend Holroyd, "never pretend to allure
me by painting in odious colours the dust of London.
I love the dust, and whenever I move into the Weald it
is to visit you, and not your trees." His ideal was to
devote the morning, commencing early—at seven, say—to
study, and the afternoon and evening to society and
recreation, not "disdaining the innocent amusement of a

game at cards." And this plan of a happy life he very
fairly realised in his little house in Bentinck Street.
The letters that we have of his relating to this period are
buoyant with spirits and self-congratulation at his happy
lot. He writes to his stepmother that he is every day
more satisfied with his present mode of life, which he
always believed was most calculated to make him happy.
The stable and moderate stimulus of congenial society,
alternating with study, was what he liked. The excitement and dissipation of a town life, which purchase
pleasure to-day at the expense of fatigue and disgust
to-morrow, were as little to his taste as the amusements
of the country. In 1772, when he settled in London,
he was young in years, but he was old in tastes, and he
enjoyed himself with the complacency often seen in
healthy old men. " My library," he writes to Holroyd
in 1773, " Kensington Gardens, and a few parties with
new acquaintance, among whom I reckon Goldsmith and
Sir Joshua Reynolds," (poor Goldsmith was to die the
year following), "fill up my time, and the monster
ennui preserves a very respectful distance. By the
by, your friends Batt, Sir John Russell, and Lascelles
dined with me one day before they set off : *for I sometimes give the prettiest little dinner in the world.*" One
can imagine Gibbon, the picture of plumpness and
content, doing the honours of his modest household.
Still he was never prominent in society, even after
the publication of his great work had made him
famous. Lord Sheffield says that his conversation was
superior to his writings, and in a circle of intimate
friends it is probable that this was true. But in the
free encounter of wit and argument, the same want of
readiness that made him silent in parliament would

most likely restrict his conversational power. It may be
doubted if there is a striking remark or saying of his
on record. His name occurs in Boswell, but nearly
always as a *persona muta*. Certainly the arena where
Johnson and Burke encountered each other was not
fitted to bring out a shy and not very quick man.
Against Johnson he manifestly harboured a sort of
grudge, and if he ever felt the weight of Ursa Major's
paw it is not surprising.

He rather oddly preserved an instance of his conver
sational skill, as if aware that he would not easily get
credit for it. The scene was in Paris. " At the table of
my old friend M. de Foncemagne, I was involved in a
dispute with the Abbé de Mably . . . As I might be
partial in my own cause, I shall transcribe the words of
an unknown critic. ' You were, my dear Théodon, at
M. de Foncemagne's house, when the Abbé de Mably and
Mr. Gibbon dined there along with a number of guests.
The conversation ran almost entirely on history. The
Abbé, being a profound politician, turned it while at
dessert on the administration of affairs, and as by genius
and temper, and the habit of admiring Livy, he values
only the republican system, he began to boast of the
excellence of republics, being well persuaded that the
learned Englishman would approve of all he said and
admire the profoundity of genius that had enabled a
Frenchman to discover all these advantages. But Mr.
Gibbon, knowing by experience the inconveniences of a
popular government, was not at all of his opinion, and
generously took up the defence of monarchy. The
Abbé wished to convince him out of Livy, and by some
arguments drawn from Plutarch in favour of the
Spartans. Mr. Gibbon, being endowed with a most

excellent memory, and having all events present to his
mind, soon got the command of the conversation. The
Abbé grew angry, they lost possession of themselves,
and said hard things of each other. The Englishman
retaining his native coolness, watched for his advantages,
and pressed the Abbé with increasing success in proportion as he was more disturbed by passion. The
conversation grew warmer, and was broken off by
M. de Foncemagne's rising from table and passing into
the parlour, where no one was tempted to renew it."

But if not brilliant in society, he was very *répandu*, and
was welcomed in the best circles. He was a member of
Boodle's, White's, Brooks's, and Almack's,[1] and "there
were few persons in the literary or political world to
whom he was a stranger." It is to be regretted that the
best sketch of him at this period borders on caricature.
"The learned Gibbon," says Colman, "was a curious
counterbalance to the learned (may I not say the less
learned) Johnson. Their manners and tastes, both in
writing and conversation, were as different as their
habiliments. On the day I first sat down with Johnson
in his rusty-brown suit and his black worsted stockings,
Gibbon was placed. opposite to me in a suit of flowered
velvet, with a bag and sword. Each had his measured
phraseology, and Johnson's famous parallel between
Dryden and Pope might be loosely parodied in reference
to himself and Gibbon. Johnson's style was grand, and
Gibbon's elegant : the stateliness of the former was
sometimes pedantic, and the latter was occasionally
finical. Johnson marched to kettledrums and trumpets,

---

[1] Not the assembly-room of that name, but a gaming-club where
the play was high. I find no evidence that Gibbon ever yielded to
the prevalent passion for gambling.

Gibbon moved to flutes and hautboys. Johnson hewed passages through the Alps, while Gibbon levelled walks through parks and gardens. Mauled as I had been by Johnson, Gibbon poured balm upon my bruises by condescending once or twice in the course of the evening to talk with me. The great historian was light and playful, suiting his matter to the capacity of the boy : but it was done *more suo*—still his mannerism prevailed, still he tapped his snuff-box, still he smirked and smiled, and rounded his periods with the same air of good-breeding, as if he were conversing with men. His mouth, mellifluous as Plato's, was a round hole nearly in the centre of his visage." (Quoted in Croker's *Boswell.*)

Now and then he even joins in a masquerade, " the finest thing ever seen," which costs two thousand guineas. But the chief charm of it to him seems to have been the pleasure that it gave to his Aunt Porten. These little vanities are however quite superficial, and are never allowed to interfere with work.

Now indeed he was no loiterer. In three years after his settlement in London he had produced the first volume of the *Decline and Fall :* an amount of diligence which will not be underrated by those who appreciate the vast difference between commencing and continuing an undertaking of that magnitude. " At the outset," he says, " all was dark and doubtful ; even the title of the work, the true æra of the decline and fall of the empire, the limits of the Introduction, the division of the chapters, and the order of the narrative,—and I was often tempted to cast away the labour of seven years ; "—alternations no doubt of hope and despair familiar to every sincere and competent

student. But he had taken the best and only reliable
means of securing himself from the danger of these
fluctuations of spirit. He finished his reading and preparation before he began to write, and when he at last
put pen to paper his course lay open before him, with no
fear of sudden and disquieting stoppages arising from
imperfect knowledge and need of further inquiry. It
is a pity that we cannot follow the elaboration of the
work in detail. That portion of his Memoirs in which
he speaks of it is very short and fragmentary, and the
defect is not supplied by his letters. He seems to have
worked with singular ease and mastery of his subject,
and never to have felt his task as a strain or a fatigue.
Even his intimate friends were not aware that he was
engaged on a work of such magnitude, and it is amusing
to see his friend Holroyd warn him against a hasty and
immature publication when he learned that the book
was in the press. He had apparently heard little of
it before. This alone would show with what ease and
smoothness Gibbon must have worked. He had excellent health—a strange fact after his sickly childhood;
society unbent his mind instead of distracting it; his
stomach was perfect—perhaps too good, as about this
time he began to be admonished by the gout. He never
seems to have needed change. "Sufficient for the
summer is the evil thereof, viz., one distant country
excursion." There was an extraordinary difference in
this respect between the present age and those which
went before it; restlessness and change of scene have
become almost a necessity of life with us, whereas our
ancestors could continue healthy and happy for months
and years without stirring from home. What is there
to explain the change? We must not pretend that we

work harder than they did.[1] However, Gibbon was
able to keep himself in good condition with his long
spell of work in the morning, and his dinner-parties
at home or elsewhere in the afternoon, and to have
kept at home as much as he could. Whenever he
went away to the country, it was on invitations which
he could not well refuse. The result was a leisurely,
unhasting fulness of achievement, calm stretches of
thorough and contented work, which have left their
marks on the *Decline and Fall*. One of its charms is
a constant good humour and complacency ; not a sign is
visible that the writer is pressed for time, or wants to
get his performance out of hand ; but, on the contrary,
a calm lingering over details, sprightly asides in the
notes, which the least hurry would have suppressed
or passed by, and a general impression conveyed of
thorough enjoyment in the immensity of the labour.

One would have liked to see this elaboration more
clearly, to have been allowed a glimpse into his workshop
while he was so engaged. Unfortunately the editor of his
journals has selected the relatively unimportant records
of his earlier studies, and left us in the dark as regards
this far more interesting period. He was such an inde-
fatigable diarist that it is unlikely that he neglected to
keep a journal in this crisis of his studies. But it has
not been published, and it may have been destroyed.
All that we have is this short paragraph in his
Memoirs :—

"The classics, as low as Tacitus and the younger Pliny and

---

[1] The most remarkable instance of all is the case of Newton,
who, according to Dr. Whewell, resided in Trinity College "for
thirty-five years without the interruption of a month."—*Hist. of
the Inductive Sciences*, vol. ii. book vii.

Juvenal, were my old and familiar companions. I insensibly plunged into the ocean of the Augustan history, and in the descending series I investigated, with my pen almost always in my hand, the original records, both Greek and Latin, from Dion Cassius to Ammianus Marcellinus, from the reign of Trajan to the last age of the Western Cæsars. The subsidiary rays of medals and inscriptions of geography and chronology, were thrown on their proper objects, and I applied the collections of Tillemont to fix and arrange within my reach the loose and scattered atoms of historical information. Through the darkness of the middle ages I explored my way in the *Annals and Antiquities of Italy* of the learned Muratori, and diligently compared them with the parallel or transverse lines of Sigonius and Maffei, Baronius and Pagi, till I almost grasped the ruins of Rome in the fourteenth century, without suspecting that this final chapter must be attained by the labour of six quartos and twenty years."

When the time for composition arrived, he showed a fastidiousness which was full of good augury. "Three times did I compose the first chapter, and twice the second and third, before I was tolerably satisfied with their effect." His hand grew firmer as he advanced. But the two final chapters interposed a long delay, and needed "three successive revisals to reduce them from a volume to their present size." Gibbon spent more time over his first volume than over any one of the five which followed it. To these he devoted almost regularly two years apiece, more or less, whereas the first cost him three years—so disproportionately difficult is the start in matters of this kind.

While engaged in the composition of the first volume, he became a member of Parliament. One morning at half past seven, "as he was destroying an army of barbarians," he heard a double rap at his door. It was a friend who came to inquire if he was desirous of

entering the House of Commons. The answer may
be imagined, and he took his seat as member for
the borough of Liskeard after the general election
in 1774.

Gibbon's political career is the side of his history from
which a friendly biographer would most readily turn
away. Not that it was exceptionally ignoble or self-
seeking if tried by the standard of the time, but it was
altogether commonplace and unworthy of him. The
fact that he never even once opened his mouth in the
House is not in itself blameworthy, though disappointing
in a man of his power. It was indeed laudable enough
if he had nothing to say. But why had he nothing to
say? His excuse is timidity and want of readiness.
We may reasonably assume that the cause lay deeper.
With his mental vigour he would soon have overcome
such obstacles if he had really wished and tried to
overcome them. The fact is that he never tried because
he never wished. It is a singular thing to say of such a
man, but nevertheless true, that he had no taste or
capacity whatever for politics. He lived at one of the
most exciting periods of our history; he assisted at
debates in which constitutional and imperial questions
of the highest moment were discussed by masters of
eloquence and state policy, and he hardly appears to
have been aware of the fact. It was not that he
despised politics as Walpole affected to do, or that he
regarded party struggles as "barbarous and absurd
faction," as Hume did; still less did he pass by them
with the supercilious indifference of a mystic whose
eyes are fixed on the individual spirit of man as the one
spring of good and evil. He never rose to the level of
the ordinary citizen or even partisan, who takes an

exaggerated view perhaps of the importance of the politics
of the day, but who at any rate thereby shows a sense of
social solidarity and the claims of civic communion.   He
called himself a Whig, but he had no zeal for Whig
principles.   He voted steadily with Lord North, and
quite approved of taxing and coercing America into
slavery ; but he had no high notions of the royal prerogative, and was lukewarm in this as in everything.
With such absence of passion one might have expected
that he would be at least shrewd and sagacious in his
judgments on politics.   But he is nothing of the kind.
In his familiar letters he reserves generally a few lines
for parliamentary gossip, amid chat about the weather
and family business.   He never approaches to a broad
survey of policy, or expresses serious and settled con-
victions on home or foreign affairs.   Throughout the
American war he never seems to have really made up
his mind on the nature of the struggle, and the momentous issues that it involved.   Favourable news puts him
in high spirits, which are promptly cooled by the an-
nouncement of reverses; not that he ever shows any
real anxiety or despondency about the commonwealth.
His opinions on the subject are at the mercy of the last
mail.   It is disappointing to find an elegant trifler like
Horace Walpole not only far more discerning in his
appreciation of such a crisis, but also far more
patriotically sensitive as to the wisdom of the means
of meeting it, than the historian of Rome.   Gibbon's
tone often amounts to levity, and he chronicles the most
serious measures with an unconcern really surprising.
" In a few days we stop the ports of New England.
I cannot write volumes : but I am more and more
convinced that with firmness all may go well : yet I

sometimes doubt." (February 8, 1775.) "Something
will be done this year ; but in the spring the force
of the country will be exerted to the utmost : Scotch
Highlanders, Irish Papists, Hanoverians, Canadians,
Indians, &c., will all in various shapes be employed."
(August 1, 1775.) "What think you of the season, of
Siberia is it not ? A pleasant campaign in America."
(January 29, 1776.) At precisely the same time the sagacious coxcomb of Strawberry Hill was writing thus :
"The times are indeed very serious. Pacification with
America is not the measure adopted. More regiments
are ordered thither, and to-morrow a plan, I fear equi-
valent to a declaration of war, is to be laid before both
Houses. They are bold ministers methinks who do not
hesitate on civil war, in which victory may bring ruin,
and disappointment endanger their heads . . . Acqui-
sition alone can make burdens palatable, and in a war
with our own colonies we must inflict instead of acquiring
them, and we cannot recover them without undoing
them. I am still to learn wisdom and experience, if
these things are not so." (Letter to Mann, January 25,
1775.) "A war with our colonies, which is now
declared, is a proof how much influence jargon has on
human actions. A war on our own trade is popular."
(February 15, 1775.) "The war with America goes on
briskly, that is as far as voting goes. A great majority
in both houses is as brave as a mob ducking a pick-
pocket. They flatter themselves they shall terrify the
colonies into submission in three months, and are
amazed to hear that there is no such probability. They
might as well have excommunicated them, and left it to
the devil to put the sentence into execution." (February
18, 1775.) Not only is Walpole's judgment wiser, but the

elements of a wise judgment were present to him in a
way in which they were not so to Gibbon. When the latter
does attempt a forecast, he shows, as might be expected,
as little penetration of the future as appreciation of the
present. Writing from Paris on August 11, 1777, when
all French society was ablaze with enthusiasm for
America, and the court just on the point of yielding to
the current, he is under no immediate apprehensions of
a war with France, and " would not be surprised if next
summer the French were to lend their cordial assistance
to England as the weaker party." The emptiness of
his letters as regards home politics perhaps admits of a
more favourable explanation, and may be owing to the
careful suppression by their editor, Lord Sheffield, of
everything of real interest. It is impossible to estimate
the weight of this consideration, but it may be great.
Still we have a sufficient number of his letters to be
able to say that on the whole they are neither thoughtful nor graphic : they give us neither pictures of events
nor insight into the times. It must be, however, remembered that Gibbon greatly disliked letter-writing,
and never wrote unless he was obliged.

It was no secret that Gibbon wanted a place under
government. Moderate as his establishment seems to
have been, it was more expensive than he could afford.
and he looked, not without warrant, to a supplement of
income from one of the rich windfalls which in that
time of sinecures were wont to refresh the spirits of
sturdy supporters of administration. He had influential
friends, and even relatives, in and near the government,
and but for his parliamentary nullity he would probably
have been provided with a comfortable berth at an
early period. But his "sincere and silent vote" was

not valuable enough to command a high price from his
patrons. Once only was he able to help them with his
pen, when he drew up, at the request of Lords
Thurlow and Weymouth, his *Mémoire Justificatif*, in
French, in which "he vindicated against the French
manifesto the justice of the British arms." It was a
service worthy of a small fee, which no doubt he received. He had to wait till 1779, when he had been five
years in Parliament, before his cousin Mr. Eliot, and
his friend Wedderburne, the Attorney-General, were
able to find him a post as one of the Lords Commissioners
of Trade and Plantations. The Board of Trade, of
which he became one of the eight members, survives
in mortal memory only from being embalmed in the
bright amber of one of Burke's great speeches. "This
board, Sir, has had both its original formation and its
regeneration in a job. In a job it was conceived, and
in a job its mother brought it forth. . . . This board is
a sort of temperate bed of influence : a sort of gently
ripening hothouse, where eight members of Parliament
receive salaries of a thousand a year for a certain given
time, in order to mature at a proper season a claim to
two thousand, granted for doing less" (*Speech on Eco-
nomical Reform*). Gibbon, with entire good humour,
acknowledges the justice of Burke's indictment, and
says he was "heard with delight, even by those whose
existence he proscribed." After all, he only enjoyed the
emolument of his office for three years, and he places
that emolument at a lower figure than Burke did. He
could not have received more than between two and
three thousand pounds of public money ; and when we
consider what manner of men have fattened on the
national purse, it would be churlish to grudge that

G

small sum to the historian of the *Decline and Fall*. The
misfortune is that, reasonably or otherwise, doubts were
raised as to Gibbon's complete straightforwardness and
honourable adhesion to party ties in accepting office.
He says himself : "My acceptance of a place provoked
some of the leaders of opposition with whom I had
lived in habits of intimacy, and I was most unjustly
accused of deserting a party in which I had never
enlisted." There is certainly no evidence that those who
were most qualified to speak, those who gave him the
place and reckoned on his vote, ever complained of want
of allegiance. On the other hand, Gibbon's own letter
to Edward Elliot, accepting the place, betrays a somewhat uneasy conscience. He owns that he was far from
approving all the past measures of the administration,
even some of those in which he himself had silently
concurred ; that he saw many capital defects in the
characters of some of the present ministers, and was
sorry that in so alarming a situation of public affairs
the country had not the assistance of several able and
honest men who were now in opposition. Still, for
various reasons, he did not consider himself in any way
implicated, and rather suspiciously concludes with an
allusion to his pecuniary difficulties and a flourish.
" The addition of the salary which is now offered will
make my situation perfectly easy, but I hope that you
will do me the justice to believe that my mind could not
be so unless I were conscious of the rectitude of my
conduct."

The strongest charge against Gibbon in reference to
this matter is asserted to come from his friend Fox, in
this odd form. " In June 1781, Mr. Fox's library came
to be sold. Amongst his other books the first volume

of Mr. Gibbon's history was brought to the hammer.
In the blank leaf of this was a note in the hand-
writing of Mr. Fox, stating a remarkable declaration of
our historian at a well-known tavern in Pall Mall, and
contrasting it with Mr. Gibbon's political conduct afterwards. 'The author,' it observed, 'at Brooks's said
that there was no salvation for this country until six
heads of the principal persons in administration' (Lord
North being then prime minister) 'were laid upon
the table. Yet,' as the observation added, 'eleven days
afterwards this same gentleman accepted a place of a
lord of trade under these very ministers, and has acted
with them ever since.'" It is impossible to tell what
amount of truth there is in this story, and not very
important to inquire. It rests on the authority of a
strong personal enemy, and the cordial intimacy which
ever subsisted between Gibbon and Fox seems to show
that it was mere calumny. Perhaps the fact that Gibbon
had really no opinions in politics may have led persons
of opposite parties to think that he agreed with them
more than he did, and when he merely followed his own
interest, they may have inferred that he was deserting
their principles. After losing his post on the Board of
Trade he still hoped for Government employ, "either a
secure seat at the Board of Customs or Excise," or in
a diplomatic capacity. He was disappointed. If Lord
Sheffield is to be believed, it was his friend Fox who
frustrated his appointment as secretary of embassy at
Paris, when he had been already named to that
office.

The way in which Gibbon acted and afterwards spoke
in reference to the celebrated Coalition gives perhaps
the best measure of his political calibre. He voted

among the rank and file of Lord North's followers for
the Coalition with meek subserviency. He speaks of
a "principle of gratitude" which actuated him on this
occasion. Lord North had given him his seat, and if a
man's conscience allows him to think rather of his
patron than of his country, there is nothing to be said,
except that his code of political ethics is low. We may
admit that his vote was pledged; but there is also no
doubt that any gratitude that there was in the matter
was stimulated by a lively sense of favours to come. The
Portland ministry had not been long in office when he
wrote in the following terms to his friend Deyverdun:
"You have not forgotten that I went into Parliament
without patriotism and without ambition, and that all
my views tended to the convenient and respectable
place of a lord of trade. This situation I at length
obtained. I possessed it for three years, from 1779 to
1782, and the net produce, which amounted to 750*l.*
sterling, augmented my income to my wants and desires.
But in the spring of last year the storm burst over
our heads. Lord North was overthrown, your humble
servant turned out, and even the Board of Trade, of
which I was a member, abolished and broken up for
ever by Mr. Burke's reform. To complete my misfor-
tunes, I still remain a member of the Lower House. At
the end of the last Parliament, Mr. Eliot withdrew his
nomination. But the favour of Lord North facilitated
my re-election, and gratitude imposed on me the duty of
making available for his service the rights which I held
in part from him. That winter we fought under the
allied standards of Lord North and Mr. Fox: we
triumphed over Lord Shelburne and the peace, and my
friend (*i.e.* Lord North) remounted his steed in the quality

of a secretary of state. Now he can easily say to me,
'It was a great deal for me, it was nothing for you;'
and in spite of the strongest assurances, I have too much
reason to allow me to have much faith. With great
genius and very respectable talents, he has now neither
the title nor the credit of prime minister; more active
colleagues carry off the most savoury morsels which
their voracious creatures immediately devour; our mis-
fortunes and reforms have diminished the number of
favours; either through pride or through indolence I am
but a bad suitor, and if at last I obtain something, it
may perhaps be on the eve of a fresh revolution, which
will in an instant snatch from me that which has cost
me so many cares and pains."

Such a letter speaks for itself. Gibbon might well
say that he entered parliament without patriotism and
without ambition. The only redeeming feature is the
almost cynical frankness with which he openly regards
politics from a personal point of view. However, it may
be pleaded that the letter was written to a bosom friend
at a moment of great depression, and when Gibbon's
pecuniary difficulties were pressing him severely. The
Coalition promised him a place, and that was enough;
the contempt for all principle which had brought it
about was not thought of. But even this minute
excuse does not apply to the way in which, years after,
when he was in comfort at Lausanne, he refers to the
subject in his Memoirs. The light in which the Coalition deserved to be regarded was clear by that time.
Yet he speaks of it, not only without blame or regret,
but contrives to cast suspicion on the motives of those
who were disgusted by it, and bestowed their allegiance
elsewhere.

" It is not the purpose of this narrative to expatiate on the
publié or secret history of the times : the schism which followed
the death of the Marquis of Rockingham, the appointment of the
Earl of Shelbourne, the resignation of Mr. Fox and his famous
coalition with Lord North. But I may assert with some degree of
assurance that in their political conflict those great antagonists
had never felt any personal animosity to each other, that their
reconciliation was easy and sincere, and that their friendship
has never been clouded by the shadow of suspicion or jealousy.
The *most violent* or *venal* of their respective followers embraced
this fair occasion of revolt, but their alliance still commanded a
majority of the House of Commons, the peace was censured,
Lord Shelbourne resigned, and the two friends knelt on the
same cushion to take the oath of secretary of state. From a
principle of gratitude I adhered to the Coalition ; my vote was
counted in the day of battle, but I was overlooked in the
division of the spoil."

From this we learn that it was only the *violent* and
the *venal* who disapproved of the Coalition. One
would like to know how Gibbon explained the fact that
at the general election of 1784 no less than one hundred
and sixty of the supporters of the Coalition lost their
seats, and that Fox's political reputation was all but
irretrievably ruined from this time forward.

Meanwhile he had not neglected his own proper
work. The first volume of his history was published in
February, 1776. It derived, he says, "more credit from
the name of the shop than from that of the author." In
the first instance he intended to print only five hundred
copies, but the number was doubled by the "prophetic
taste" of his printer, Mr. Strahan. The book was
received with a burst of applause—it was a *succès fou.*
The first impression was exhausted in a few days, and
a second and third edition were scarcely adequate to the

demand. The wiser few were as warm in their eulogies
as the general public. • Hume declared that if he had
not been personally acquainted with the author, he
should have been surprised by such a performance
coming from any Englishman in that age. Dr. Robertson, Adam Ferguson, and Horace Walpole joined in
the chorus. Walpole betrays an amusing mixture of
admiration and pique at not having found the author
out before. " I know him a little, and never suspected
the extent of his talents ; for he is perfectly modest, or
I want penetration, which I know too ; but I intend to
know him a great deal more." He oddly enough says
that Gibbon was the " son of a foolish alderman," which
shows at least how little the author was known in the
great world up to this time. Now, however, society
was determined to know more of him, the surest
proof, not of merit, but of success. It must have
been a rather intoxicating moment, but Gibbon had
a cool head not easily turned. It would be unfair not
to add that he had something much better, a really
warm and affectionate regard for old friends, the best
preservative against the fumes of flattery and sudden
fame. Holroyd, Deyverdun, Madame Necker were more
to him than all the great people with whom he now became acquainted. Necker and his wife came over from
Paris and paid him a long visit in Bentinck Street, when
his laurels were just fresh. " I live with her " he writes,
" just as I used to do twenty years ago, laugh at her Paris
varnish, and oblige her to become a simple reasonable
Suissesse. The man, who might read English husbands
lessons of proper and dutiful behaviour, is a sensible,
good-natured creature." The next year he returned
the visit to Paris. His fame had preceded him, and he

received the cordial but discriminating welcome which
the *ancien régime* at that time specially reserved for *gens
d'esprit.* Madame du Deffand writes to Walpole, "Mr.
Gibbon has the greatest success here ; it is quite a struggle
to get him." He did not deny himself a rather sumptuous
style of living while in Paris. Perhaps the recollection
of the unpleasant effect of his English clothes and the
long waists of the French on his former visit dwelt
in his mind, for now, like Walpole, he procured a new
outfit at once. "After decking myself out with silks
and silver, the ordinary establishment of coach, lodgings,
servants, eating, and pocket expenses, does not exceed
60*l.* per month. Yet I have two footmen in handsome
liveries behind my coach, and my apartment is hung
with damask."

The remainder of his life in London has nothing important. He persevered assiduously with his history,
and had two more quartos ready in 1781. They were
received with less enthusiasm than the first, although
they were really superior. Gibbon was rather too
modestly inclined to agree with the public and "to
believe that, especially in the beginning, they were more
prolix and less entertaining " than the previous volume.
He also wasted some weeks on his vindication of the
fifteenth and sixteenth chapters of that volume, which
had excited a host of feeble and ill-mannered attacks.
His defence was complete, and in excellent temper. But
the piece has no permanent value. His assailants were
so ignorant and silly that they gave no scope for a great
controversial reply. Neither perhaps did the subject
admit of it. A literary war generally makes people
think of Bentley's incomparable *Phalaris.* But that
was almost a unique occasion and victory in the history

of letters. Bentley himself, the most pugnacious of men, never found such another.

And so the time glided by, till we come to the year 1783. Lord North had resigned office, the Board of Trade was abolished, and Gibbon had lost his convenient salary. The outlook was not pleasant. The seat on the Board of Customs or Excise with which his hopes had been for a time kept up, receded into a remote distance, and he came to the conclusion " that the reign of pensions and sinecures was at an end." It was clearly necessary to take some important step in the way of retrenchment. After he had lost his official income, his expenses exceeded his revenue by something like four hundred pounds. A less expensive style of living in London never seems to have presented itself as an alternative. So, like many an Englishman before and since, he resolved to go abroad to economise.

His old friend Deyverdun was now settled in a comfortable house at Lausanne, overlooking the Lake of Geneva. They had not met for eight years. But the friendship had begun a quarter of a century before, in the old days when Gibbon was a boarder in Pavillard's house, and the embers of old associations only wanted stirring to make them shoot up into flame. In a moment of expansion Gibbon wrote off a warm and eager letter to his friend, setting forth his unsatisfactory position, and his wish and even necessity to change it. He gradually and with much delicacy discloses his plan, that he and Deyverdun, both now old bachelors, should combine their solitary lives in a common household and carry out an old project, often discussed in younger days, of living together. " You live in a charming house. I see from here my apartment, the rooms we shall share with one another, our table, our walks. But such a marriage is worthless unless it suits both parties, and I easily feel that circumstances, new tastes, and connections may frustrate a design which appeared charming in the distance. To settle my mind and to avoid regrets, you must be as frank as I have been, and give me a true picture, external and internal, of George Deyverdun."

This letter, written in fluent and perfect French, is one of the best that we have of Gibbon. Deyverdun answered promptly, and met his friend's advances with at least equal warmth. The few letters that have been preserved of his connected with this subject give a highly favourable idea of his mind and character, and show he was quite worthy of the long and constant attachment that Gibbon felt for him. He cannot express the delight he has felt at his friend's proposal; by the rarest piece of good fortune, it so happens that he himself is in a somewhat similar position of uncertainty and difficulty; a year ago Gibbon's letter would have given him pleasure, now it offers assistance and support. After a few details concerning the tenant who occupies a portion of his house, he proceeds to urge Gibbon to carry out the project he had suggested, to break loose from parliament and politics, for which he was not fit, and to give himself up to the charms of study and friendship. "Call to mind, my dear friend," he goes on, "that I saw you enter parliament with regret, and I think I was only too good a prophet. I am sure that career has caused you more privations than joys, more pains than pleasures. Ever since I have known you I have been convinced that your happiness lay in your study and in society, and that any path which led you

elsewhere was a departure from happiness." Through
nine pages of gentle and friendly eloquence Deyverdun
pursues his argument to induce his friend to clinch the
bargain. " I advise you not only not to solicit a place,
but to refuse one if it were offered to you. Would a
thousand a year make up to you for the loss of five days
a week? . . . . By making this retreat to Switzerland,
besides the beauty of the country and the pleasures of
its society, you will acquire two blessings which you
have lost, liberty and competence. You will also be
useful, your works will continue to enlighten us, and,
independently of your talents, the man of honour and
refinement is never useless." He then skilfully ex-
hibits the attractions he has to offer. " You used to
like my house and garden ; what would you do now?
On the first floor, which looks on the declivity of Ouchy,
I have fitted up an apartment which is enough for me.
I have a servant's room, two *salons*, two cabinets. On
a level with the terrace two other *salons*, of which one
serves as a dining-room in summer, and the other a
drawing-room for company. I have arranged three
more rooms between the house and the coachhouse, so
that I can offer you all the large apartment, which consists actually of eleven rooms, great and small, looking
east and south, not splendidly furnished, I allow, but
with a certain elegance which I hope you will like. The
terrace is but little altered . . . . it is lined from end
to end with boxes of orange-trees. The vine-trellis has
prospered, and extends nearly to the end. I have purchased the vineyard below the garden, and in front of
the house made it into a lawn, which is watered by the
water of the fountain . . . . In a word, strangers come
to see the place, and in spite of my pompous description

of it I think you will like it .... If you come,
you will find a tranquillity which you cannot have
in London, and a friend who has not passed a single
day without thinking of you, and who, in spite of his
defects, his foibles, and his inferiority, is still one of
the companions who suits you best."

More letters followed from both sides in a similar
strain. Yet Gibbon quailed before a final resolution.
His aunt, Mrs. Porten, his mother, Mrs. Gibbon, his
friend, Lord Sheffield, all joined in deprecating his
voluntary exile. "That is a nonsensical scheme," said
the latter, "you have got into your head of returning to
Lausanne—a pretty fancy; you remember how much
you liked it in your youth, but now you have seen more
of the world, and if you were to try it again you would
find yourself woefully disappointed." Deyverdun, with
complete sympathy, begged him not to be in too great
a hurry to decide on a course which he himself desired
so much. "I agree with you," he wrote to Gibbon,
"that this is a sort of marriage, but I could never forgive
myself if I saw you dissatisfied in the sequel, and in a
position to reproach me." Gibbon felt it was a case
demanding decision of character, and he came to a
determination with a promptitude and energy not usual
with him. He promised Deyverdun in the next letter
an ultimatum, stating whether he meant to *go* or to *stay*,
and a week after he wrote, "I go." He had prudently
refrained from consulting Lord Sheffield during this
critical period, knowing that his certain disapprobation
of the scheme would only complicate matters and
render decision more difficult. Then he wrote, "I have
given Deyverdun my word of honour to be at Lausanne
at the beginning of October, and no power of persuasion

can divert me from this *irrevocable* resolution, which
I am every day proceeding to execute."

This was no exaggeration. He cancelled the lease of
his house in Bentinck Street, packed the more necessary
portion of his books and shipped them for Rouen, and as
his postchaise moved over Westminster Bridge, "bade a
long farewell to the *fumum et opes strepitumque Romæ.*"
The only real pang he felt in leaving arose from the
"silent grief" of his Aunt Porten, whom he did not hope
to see again. Nor did he. He started on September
15, 1783, slept at Dover, was flattered with the hope of
making Calais harbour by the same tide in "three hours
and a half, as the wind was brisk and fair," but was
driven into Boulogne. He had not a symptom of sea
sickness. Then he went on by easy stages through
Aire, Bethune, Douay, Cambray, St. Quentin, La Fère,
Laon, Rheims, Chalons, St. Dizier, Langres, Besançon,
and arrived at Lausanne on the 27th. The inns he
found more agreeable to the palate than to the sight or
the smell. At Langres he had an excellent bed about
six feet high from the ground. He beguiled the time
with Homer and Clarendon, talking with his servant,
Caplin, and his dog Muff, and sometimes with the
French postilions, and he found them the least rational
of the animals mentioned.

He reached his journey's end, to alight amid a number of minor troubles, which to a less easy tempered
man would have been real annoyances. He found that
Deyverdun had reckoned without his host, or rather his
tenant, and that they could not have possession of the
house for several months, so he had to take lodgings.
Then he sprained his ankle, and this brought on a bad
attack of the gout, which laid him up completely.

However, his spirits never gave way. In time his books arrived, and the friends got installed in their own house. His satisfaction has then no bounds, with the people, the place, the way of living, and his daily companion. We must now leave him for a short space in the enjoyment of his happiness, while we briefly consider the labours of the previous ten years.

CHAPTER VII.

THE FIRST THREE VOLUMES OF THE DECLINE AND FALL.

THE historian who is also an artist is exposed to a particular drawback from which his brethren in other fields are exempt. The mere lapse of time destroys the value and even the fidelity of his pictures. In other arts correct colouring and outline remain correct, and if they are combined with imaginative power, age rather enhances than diminishes their worth. But the historian lives under another law. His reproduction of a past age, however full and true it may appear to his contemporaries, appears less and less true to his successors. The way in which he saw things ceases to be satisfactory; we may admit his accuracy, but we add a qualification referring to the time when he wrote, the point of view that he occupied. And we feel that what was accurate for him is no longer accurate for us. This superannuation of historical work is not similar to the superseding of scientific work which is ever going on, and is the capital test of progress. Scientific books become rapidly old-fashioned, because the science to which they refer is in constant growth, and a work on chemistry or biology is out of date by reason of incompleteness

or the discovery of unsuspected errors. The scientific
side of history, if we allow it to have a scientific side,
conforms to this rule, and presents no singularity.
Closer inspection of our materials, the employment
of the comparative method, occasionally the bringing
to light of new authorities—all contribute to an
increase of real knowledge, and historical studies in
this respect do not differ from other branches of research. But this is not the sole or the chief cause of
the renovation and transformation constantly needed in
historic work. That depends on the ever-moving standpoint from which the past is regarded, so that society in
looking back on its previous history never sees it for
long together at quite the same angle, never sees, we
may say, quite the same thing. The past changes to us
as we move down the stream of time, as a distant mountain changes through the windings of the road on which
we travel away from it. To drop figure and use language
now becoming familiar, the social organism is in constant
growth, and receiving new additions, and each new addition causes us to modify our view of the whole. The
historian, in fact, is engaged in the study of an unfinished organism, whose development is constantly pre-
senting him with surprises. It is as if the biologist
were suddenly to come upon new and unheard-of species
and families which would upset his old classification, or
as if the chemist were to find his laws of combination
replaced by others which were not only unknown to him,
but which were really new and recent in the world.
Other inquirers have the whole of the phenomena with
which their science is concerned before them, and they
may explore them at their leisure. The sociologist has
only an instalment, most likely a very small instalment,

of the phenomena with which his science is concerned
before him. They have not yet happened, are not
yet phenomena, and as they do happen and admit of
investigation they necessarily lead to constant modifica-
tion of his views and deductions. Not only does he
acquire new knowledge like other inquirers, but he is
constantly having the subject-matter from which he
derives his knowledge augmented. Even in modern
times society has thrown out with much sudden-
ness rapid and unexpected developments, of such scope
and volume that contemporaries have often lost self-
possession at the sight of them, and wondered if social
order could survive. The Reformation and the French
Revolution are cases in point. And what a principal part
do these two great events always play in any specu-
lations instituted subsequent to them! How easy it is
to see whether a writer lived before the Reign of Terror,
or after it, from his gait and manner of approaching
social inquiries! Is there any reason to suppose that
such mutations are now at an end? None. The probability, well nigh a certainty, is that metamorphoses of
the social organism are in store for us which will equal,
if they do not vastly exceed, anything that the past has
offered.

Considerations of this kind need to be kept in view
if we would be just in our appreciation of historical
writings which have already a certain age. It is impossible that a history composed a century ago should
fully satisfy us now; but we must beware of blaming
the writer for his supposed or real shortcomings, till we
have ascertained how far they arose from his personal
inadequacy to his task, and were not the result of his

H

chronological position. It need not be said that this
remark does not refer to many books which are called
histories, but are really contemporary memoirs and
original authorities subservient to history proper. The
works of Clarendon and Burnet, for instance, can never
lose a certain value on this account. The immortal
book which all subsequent generations have agreed to
call a possession for ever, is the unapproachable ideal of
this class. But neither Thucydides nor Clarendon were
historians in the sense in which Gibbon was an historian,
that is, engaged in the delineation of a remote epoch by
the help of such materials as have escaped the ravages
of time. It is historians like Gibbon who are exposed
to the particular unhappiness referred to a little way
back—that of growing out of date through no fault of
their own, but through the changed aspect presented
by the past in consequence of the movement which has
brought us to the present. But if this is the field of historical disaster, it is also the opportunity of historical
genius. In proportion as a writer transcends the special
limitations of his time, will "age fail to wither him."
That he cannot entirely shake off the fetters which
fasten him to his epoch is manifest. But in proportion as his vision is clear, in proportion as he has
with singleness of eye striven to draw the past with
reverent loyalty, will his bondage to his own time be
loosened, and his work will remain faithful work for
which due gratitude will not be withheld.

The sudden and rapid expansion of historic studies
in the middle of the eighteenth century constitutes one
of the great epochs in literature. Up to the year 1750
no great historical work had appeared in any modern

language.[1] The instances that seem to make against
this remark will be found to confirm it. They consist
of memoirs, contemporary documents, in short materials
for history, but not history itself. From Froissart and
De Comines, or even from the earlier monastic writers
to St. Simon (who was just finishing his incomparable
Memoirs), history with wide outlook and the conception
of social progress and interconnection of events did not
exist. Yet history in its simple forms is one of the
most spontaneous of human achievements. Stories of
mighty deeds, of the prowess and death of heroes, are
among the earliest productions of even semi-civilised
man—the earliest subjects of epic and lyric verse.
But this rudimentary form is never more than biogra-
phical. With increasing complexity of social evolution
it dies away, and history proper, as distinct from annals
and chronicle, does not arise till circumstances allow of
general and synthetic views, till societies can be surveyed from a sufficient distance and elevation for their
movements to be discerned. Thucydides, Livy, and
Tacitus do not appear till Greece and Rome have reached
their highest point of homogeneous national life. The
tardy dawn of history in the modern world was owing
to its immense complexity. Materials also were wanting. They gradually emerged out of manuscript all over
Europe, during what may be called the great pedant
age (1550-1650), under the direction of meritorious an-
tiquaries, Camden, Savile, Duchesne, Gale, and others.
Still official documents and state papers were wanting,
and had they been at hand would hardly have been

---

[1] Mézeray's great history of France is next to valueless till he
reaches the sixteenth century, that was a period bordering on his
own. Thuanus deals with contemporary events.

used with competence. The national and religious
limitations were still too marked and hostile to permit
a free survey over the historic field. The eighteenth
century, though it opened with a bloody war, was essentially peaceful in spirit : governments made war, but
men and nations longed for rest. The increased interest in the past was shown by the publication nearly
contemporary of the great historic collections of Rymer
(A.D. 1704), Leibnitz (1707), and Muratori (1723).
Before the middle of the century the historic muse had
abundant oil to feed her lamp. Still the lamp would
probably not have been lighted but for the singular
pass to which French thought had come.

From the latter years of Louis XIV. till the third
quarter of the eighteenth century was all but closed,
France had a government at once so weak and wicked,
so much below the culture of the people it oppressed,
that the better minds of the nation turned away in disgust from their domestic ignominy, and sought consola-
tion in contemplating foreign virtue wherever they
thought it was to be found; in short, they became
cosmopolitan. The country which has since been the
birthplace of Chauvinism, put away national pride almost
with passion. But this was not all. The country whose
king was called the Eldest Son of the Church, and with
which untold pains had been taken to keep it orthodox,
had lapsed into such an abhorrence of the Church and
of orthodoxy that anything seemed preferable to them
in its eyes.

Thus, as if by enchantment, the old barriers disappeared, both national and religious. Man and his
fortunes, in all climes and all ages, became topics of
intense interest, especially when they tended to degrade

by contrast the detested condition of things at home.
This was the weak side of historical speculation in
France : it was essentially polemical ; prompted less by
genuine interest in the past than by strong hatred of
the present. Of this perturbation note must be taken.
But it is none the less true that the disengagement of
French thought from the narrow limits of nation and
creed produced, as it were in a moment, a lofty conception of history such as subsequent ages may equal, but
can hardly surpass.

The influence of French thought was European, and
nowhere more beneficial than in England. In other
countries it was too despotic, and produced in Germany,
at least, Lessing's memorable reaction. But the robust
national and political life of England reduced it to a
welcome flavouring of our insular temperament. The
Scotch, who had a traditional connection with France,
were the first importers of the new views. Hume, who
had practically grown in the same soil as Voltaire, was
only three years behind him in the historic field. The
Age of Louis XIV. was published in 1751, and the first
volume of the *History of England* in 1754. Hume was
no disciple of Voltaire ; he simply wrote under the
stimulus of the same order of ideas. Robertson, who
shortly followed him, no doubt drew direct inspiration
from Voltaire, and his weightiest achievement, the
View of the State of Europe, prefixed to his *History of
Charles V.*, was largely influenced, if it was not absolutely suggested, by the *Essay on Manners.* But both
Hume and Robertson surpassed their masters, if we
allow, as seems right, that the French were their
masters. The Scotch writers had no quarrel with their
country or their age as the French had. One was a

Tory, the other a Whig; and Hume allowed himself to
be unworthily affected by party bias in his historical
judgment. But neither was tempted to turn history
into a covert attack on the condition of things amid
which they lived. Hence a calmness and dignity of
tone and language, very different from the petulant
brilliancy of Voltaire, who is never so happy as when
he can make the past look mean and ridiculous, merely
because it was the parent of the odious present. But,
excellent as were the Scotch historians—Hume, in style
nearly perfect; Robertson, admirable for gravity and
shrewd sense—they yet left much to be desired. Hume
had despatched his five quartos, containing the whole
history of England from the Roman period to the
Revolution, in nine years. Considering that the subject
was new to him when he began, such rapidity made
genuine research out of the question. Robertson had
the oddest way of consulting his friends as to what
subject it would be advisable for him to treat, and was
open to proposals from any quarter with exemplary
impartiality; this only showed how little the stern
conditions of real historic inquiry were appreciated by
him. In fact it is not doing them injustice to say that
these eminent men were a sort of modern Livies, chiefly
occupied with the rhetorical part of their work, and not
over inclined to waste their time in ungrateful digging
in the deep mines of historic lore. Obviously the place
was open for a writer who should unite all the broad
spirit of comprehensive survey, with the thorough and
minute patience of a Benedictine; whose subject, mel-
lowed by long brooding, should have sought him rather
than he it; whose whole previous course of study had
been an unconscious preparation for one great effort

which was to fill his life. When Gibbon sat down to
write his book, the man had been found who united
these difficult conditions.

The decline and fall of Rome is the greatest event in
history. It occupied a larger portion of the earth's
surface, it affected the lives and fortunes of a larger
number of human beings, than any other revolution on
record. For it was essentially one, though it took
centuries to consummate, and though it had for its
theatre the civilised world. Great evolutions and
catastrophes happened before it, and have happened
since, but nothing which can compare with it in volume
and mere physical size. Nor was it less morally. The
destruction of Rome was not only a destruction of an
empire, it was the destruction of a phase of human
thought, of a system of human beliefs, of morals,
politics, civilisation, as all these had existed in the
world for ages. The drama is so vast, the cataclysm so
appalling, that even at this day we are hardly removed
from it far enough to take it fully in. The mind is oppressed, the imagination flags under the load imposed
upon it. The capture and sack of a town one can
fairly conceive: the massacre, outrage, the flaming roofs,
the desolation. Even the devastation of a province
can be approximately reproduced in thought. But
what thought can embrace the devastation and destruction of all the civilised portions of Europe, Africa, and
Asia? Who can realise a Thirty Years War lasting
five hundred years? a devastation of the Palatinate
extending through fifteen generations? If we try to
insert into the picture, as we undoubtedly should do,
the founding of the new, which was going on beside this
destruction of the old, the settling down of the barba-

rian hosts in the conquered provinces, the expansion of
the victorious Church, driving paganism from the towns
to the country and at last extinguishing it entirely, the
effort becomes more difficult than ever. The legend of
the Seven Sleepers testifies to the need men felt, even
before the tragedy had come to an end, to symbolize in
a manageable form the tremendous changes they saw
going on around them. But the legend only refers to
the changes in religion. The fall of Rome was much
more than that. It was the death of the old pagan
world and the birth of the new Christian world—the
greatest transition in history.

This, and no less than this, is Gibbon's subject.

He has treated it in such a way as even now fills competent judges with something like astonishment. His
accuracy, coupled with the extraordinary range of his
matter, the variety of his topics, the complexity of his
undertaking, the fulness and thoroughness of his knowledge, never failing at any point over the vast field, the
ease and mastery with which he lifts the enormous load,
are appreciated in proportion to the information and
abilities of his critic. One testimonial will suffice.
Mr. Freeman says : " That Gibbon should ever be dis-
placed seems impossible. That wonderful man mono-
polised, so to speak, the historical genius and the
historical learning of a whole generation, and left little,
indeed, of either for his contemporaries. He remains
the one historian of the eighteenth century whom
modern research has neither set aside nor threatened to
set aside. We may correct and improve from the stores
which have been opened since Gibbon's time ; we may
write again large parts of his story from other and often
truer and more wholesome points of view, but the work

of Gibbon as a whole, as the encyclopædic history of
1300 years, as the grandest of historical designs, carried
out alike with wonderful power and with wonderful
accuracy, must ever keep its place. Whatever else is
read, Gibbon must be read too."

Gibbon's immense scheme did not unfold itself to him
at once : he passed through at least two distinct stages
in the conception of his work. The original idea had
been confined to the decline and fall of the city of
Rome. Before he began to write, this had been
expanded to the fall of the empire of the West.
The first volume, which we saw him publish in the
last chapter, was only an instalment, limited to the
accession of Constantine, through a doubt as to how
his labours would be received. The two following
volumes, published in 1781, completed his primitive
plan. Then he paused exactly a year before he resolved
to carry on his work to its true end, the taking of
Constantinople by the Turks in 1453. The latter portion he achieved in three volumes more, which he gave
to the world on his fifty-first birthday, in 1788. Thus
the work naturally falls into two equal parts. It will
be more convenient to disregard in our remarks the
interval of five years which separated the publication of
the first volume from its two immediate companions.
The first three volumes constitute a whole in themselves,
which we will now consider.

From the accession cf Commodus, A.D. 180, to the
last of the Western Cæsars, A.D. 476, three centuries
elapsed. The first date is a real point of departure,
the commencement of a new stage of decay in the empire. The second is a mere official record of the final
disappearance of a series of phantom sovereigns, whose

vanishing was hardly noticed. Between these limits the
empire passed from the autumnal calm of the Antonine
period, through the dreadful century of anarchy between
Pertinax and Diocletian, through the relative peace
brought about by Diocletian's reforms, the civil wars of
the sons of Constantine, the disastrous defeat of Julian,
the calamities of the Gothic war, the short respite under
Theodosius, the growing anarchy and misery under his in-
competent sons, the three sieges of Rome and its sack by
the Goths, the awful appearance of Attila and his Huns,
the final submergence of the Western Empire under the
barbarians, and the universal ruin which marked the
close of the fifth century. This was the temporal side
of affairs. On the spiritual, we have the silent occult
growth of the early Church, the conversion of Constantine, the tremendous conflict of hostile sects, the heresy
of Arius, the final triumph of Athanasius, the spread
of monasticism, the extinction of paganism. Antiquity
has ended, the middle ages have begun.

Over all this immense field Gibbon moves with a
striking attitude of power, which arose from his con-
sciousness of complete preparation. What there was
to be known of his subject he felt sure that he knew.
His method of treatment is very simple, one might say
primitive, but it is very effective. He masters his materials, and then condenses and clarifies them into a broad,
well-filled narrative, which is always or nearly always
perfectly lucid through his skill in grouping events and
characters, and his fine boldness in neglecting chronological sequence for the sake of clearness and unity of action.
It is doing the book injustice to consult it only as a work
of reference, or even to read it in detached portions.
It should be read through, if we would appreciate the

art with which the story is told.   No part can be
fairly judged without regard to the remainder.   In fact,
Gibbon was much more an artist than perhaps be
suspected, and less of a philosophic thinker on history
than he would have been willing to allow.   His shortcomings in this latter respect will be adverted to
presently ; we are now considering his merits.   And
among these the very high one of lofty and vigorous
narrative stands pre-eminent.   The campaigns of Julian,
Belisarius, and Heraclius are painted with a dash and
clearness which few civil historians have equalled.
His descriptive power is also very great.   The picture
of Constantinople in the seventeenth chapter is, as the
writer of these pages can testify, a wonderful achievement, both for fidelity and brilliancy, coming from a
man who had never seen the place.

"If we survey Byzantium in the extent which it acquired
with the august name of Constantinople, the figure of the
imperial city may be represented under that of an unequal
triangle.   The obtuse point, which advances towards the east and
the shores of Asia, meets and repels the waves of the Thracian
Bosphorus.   The northern side of the city is bounded by the
harbour ; and the southern is washed by the Propontis, or Sea
of Marmora.   The basis of the triangle is opposed to the west, and
terminates the continent of Europe.   But the admirable form and
division of the circumjacent land and water cannot, without a
more ample explanation, be clearly or sufficiently understood.

"The winding channel through which the waters of the Euxine
flow with rapid and incessant course towards the Mediterranean
received the appellation of Bosphorus, a name not less celebrated
in the history than in the fables of antiquity.   A crowd of
temples and of votive altars, profusely scattered along its steep
and woody banks, attested the unskilfulness, the terrors, and
the devotion of the Grecian navigators, who, after the example
of the Argonauts, explored the dangers of the inhospitable

Euxine. On these banks tradition long preserved the memory
of the palace of Phineus, infested by the obscene Harpies, and
of the sylvan reign of Amycus, who defied the son of Leda to
the combat of the cestus. The straits of the Bosphorus are
terminated by the Cyanean rocks, which, according to the
description of the poets, had once floated on the surface of the
waters, and were destined by the gods to protect the entrance
of the Euxine against the eye of profane curiosity. From the
Cyanean rocks to the point and harbour of Byzantium the
winding length of the Bosphorus extends about sixteen miles,
and its most ordinary breadth may be computed at about one
mile and a half. The *new* castles of Europe and Asia are constructed on either continent upon the foundations of two
celebrated temples of Serapis and Jupiter Urius. The *old*
castles, a work of the Greek emperors, command the narrowest
part of the channel, in a place where the opposite banks advance
within five hundred yards of each other. These fortresses were
destroyed and strengthened by Mahomet the Second when he
meditated the siege of Constantinople ; but the Turkish conqueror was most probably ignorant that near two thousand
years before his reign Darius had chosen the same situation to
connect the two continents by a bridge of boats. At a small
distance from the old castles we discover the little town of
Chrysopolis or Scutari, which may almost be considered as the
Asiatic suburb of Constantinople. The Bosphorus, as it begins
to open into the Propontis, passes between Byzantium and
Chalcedon. The latter of these two cities was built by the
Greeks a few years before the former, and the blindness of its
founders, who overlooked the superior advantages of the opposite
coast, has been stigmatised by a proverbial expression of contempt.
  " The harbour of Constantinople, which may be considered as
an arm of the Bosphorus, obtained in a very remote period, the
denomination of the *Golden Horn*. The curve which it describes
might be compared to the horn of a stag, or as it should seem
with more propriety, to that of an ox. The epithet of *golden*
was expressive of the riches which every wind wafted from the
most distant countries into the secure and capacious port of
Constantinople. The river Lycus, formed by the conflux of two
little streams, pours into the harbour a perpetual supply of fresh

water, which serves to cleanse the bottom and to invite the periodical shoals of fish to seek their retreat in that convenient recess. As the vicissitudes of the tides are scarcely felt in those seas, the constant depth of the harbour allows goods to be landed on the quays without the assistance of boats, and it has been observed that in many places the largest vessels may rest their prows against the houses while their sterns are floating in the water. From the mouth of the Lycus to that of the harbour, this arm of the Bosphorus is more than seven miles in length. The entrance is about five hundred yards broad, and a strong chain could be occasionally drawn across it, to guard the port and the city from the attack of an hostile navy.

" Between the Bosphorus and the Hellespont, the shores of Europe and Asia receding on either side include the Sea of Marmora, which was known to the ancients by the denomination of the Propontis. The navigation from the issue of the Bosphorus to the entrance of the Hellespont is about one hundred and twenty miles. Those who steer their westward course through the middle of the Propontis may at once descry the highlands of Thrace and Bithynia and never lose sight of the lofty summit of Mount Olympus, covered with eternal snows. They leave on the left a deep gulf, at the bottom of which Nicomedia was seated, the imperial residence of Diocletian, and they pass the small islands of Cyzicus and Proconnesus before they cast anchor at Gallipoli, where the sea which separates Asia from Europe is again contracted to a narrow channel.

" The geographers, who with the most skilful accuracy have surveyed the form and extent of the Hellespont, assign about sixty miles for the winding course and about three miles for the ordinary breadth of those celebrated straits. But the narrowest part of the channel is found to the northward of the old Turkish castles between the cities of Sestos and Abydos. It was here that the adventurous Leander braved the passage of the flood for the possession of his mistress. It was here, likewise, in a place where the distance between the opposite banks cannot exceed five hundred paces, that Xerxes imposed a stupendous bridge of boats for the purpose of transporting into Europe an hundred and seventy myriads of barbarians. A sea contracted

within such narrow limits may seem but ill to deserve the
singular epithet of *broad*, which Homer, as well as Orpheus,
has frequently bestowed on the Hellespont. But our ideas of
greatness are of a relative nature ; the traveller, and especially
the poet, who sailed along the Hellespont, who pursued the windings of the stream and contemplated the rural scenery which
appeared on every side to terminate the prospect, insensibly
lost the remembrance of the sea, and his fancy painted those
celebrated straits with all the attributes of a mighty river
flowing with a swift current in the midst of a woody and inland
country, and at length through a wide mouth discharging itself
into the Ægean or Archipelago. Ancient Troy, seated on an
eminence at the foot of Mount Ida, overlooked the mouth of
the Hellespont, which scarcely received an accession of waters
from the tribute of those immortal rivulets the Simois and
Scamander. The Grecian camp had stretched twelve miles
along the shore from the Sigæan to the Rhætian promontory,
and the flanks of the army were guarded by the bravest chiefs
who fought under the banners of Agamemnon. The first of
these promontories was occupied by Achilles with his invincible
Myrmidons, and the dauntless Ajax pitched his tents on the
other. After Ajax had fallen a sacrifice to his disappointed
pride and to the ingratitude of the Greeks, his sepulchre was
erected on the ground where he had defended the navy against
the rage of Jove and Hector, and the citizens of the rising
town of Rhætium celebrated his memory with divine honours.
Before Constantine gave a just preference to the situation of
Byzantium he had conceived the design of erecting the seat of
empire on this celebrated spot, from whence the Romans derived
their fabulous origin. The extensive plain which lies below
ancient Troy towards the Rhætian promontory was first chosen
for his new capital ; and though the undertaking was soon
relinquished, the stately remains of unfinished walls and towers
attracted the notice of all who sailed through the straits of the
Hellespont.

" We are at present qualified to view the advantageous
position of Constantinople ; which appears to have been formed
by nature for the centre and capital of a great monarchy.

Situated in the forty-first degree of latitude, the imperial city commanded from her seven hills the opposite shores of Europe and Asia; the climate was healthy and temperate; the soil fertile; the harbour secure and capacious; and the approach on the side of the continent was of small extent and easy defence. The Bosphorus and the Hellespont may be considered as the two gates of Constantinople, and the prince who possesses those important passages could always shut them against a naval enemy and open them to the fleets of commerce. The preservation of the eastern provinces may in some degree be ascribed to the policy of Constantine, as the barbarians of the Euxine, who in the preceding age had poured their armaments into the heart of the Mediterranean, soon desisted from the exercise of piracy, and despaired of forcing this insurmountable barrier. When the gates of the Hellespont and Bosphorus were shut, the capital still enjoyed within their spacious inclosure every production which could supply the wants or gratify the luxury of its numerous inhabitants. The sea-coasts of Thrace and Bithynia, which languish under the weight of Turkish oppression, still exhibit a rich prospect of vineyards, of gardens, and of plentiful harvests; and the Propontis has ever been renowned for an inexhaustible store of the most exquisite fish that are taken in their stated seasons without skill and almost without labour. But when the passages of the straits were thrown open for trade, they alternately admitted the natural and artificial riches of the north and south, of the Euxine and the Mediterranean. Whatever rude commodities were collected in the forests of Germany and Scythia, and as far as the sources of the Tanais and Borysthenes; whatsoever was manufactured by the skill of Europe or Asia, the corn of Egypt, the gems and spices of the furthest India, were brought by the varying winds into the port of Constantinople, which for many ages attracted the commerce of the ancient world.

" The prospect of beauty, of safety, and of wealth united in a single spot was sufficient to justify the choice of Constantine. But as some mixture of prodigy and fable has in every age been supposed to reflect a becoming majesty on the origin of great

cities, the emperor was desirous of ascribing his resolution not
so much to the uncertain counsels of human policy as to the
eternal and infallible decrees of divine wisdom.   In one of his
laws he has been careful to instruct posterity that in obedience
to the commands of God he laid the everlasting foundations of
Constantinople, and though he has not condescended to relate
in what manner the celestial inspiration was communicated to
his mind, the defect of his modest silence has been liberally
supplied by the ingenuity of succeeding writers, who describe
the nocturnal vision which appeared to the fancy of Constantine
as he slept within the walls of Byzantium.   The tutelar genius
of the city, a venerable matron sinking under the weight of
years and infirmities, was suddenly transformed into a blooming
maid, whom his own hands adorned with all the symbols of
imperial greatness.   The monarch awoke, interpreted the au-
spicious omen, and obeyed without hesitation the will of Heaven.
The day which gave birth to a city or a colony was celebrated
by the Romans with such ceremonies as had been ordained by
a generous superstition : and though Constantine might omit
some rites which savoured too strongly of their pagan origin,
yet he was anxious to leave a deep impression of hope and
respect on the minds of the spectators.   On foot, with a lance
in his hand, the emperor himself led the solemn procession :
and directed the line which was traced as the boundary of the
destined capital : till the growing circumference was observed
with astonishment by the assistants, who at length ventured to
observe that he had already exceeded the most ample measure
of a great city. 'I shall still advance,' replied Constantine, 'till
HE, the invisible Guide who marches before me, thinks proper
to stop.' "

Gibbon proceeds to describe the extent, limits, and
edifices of Constantinople. Unfortunately the limits of
our space prevent us from giving more than a portion
of his brilliant picture.

" In the actual state of the city the palace and gardens of the
Seraglio occupy the eastern promontory, the first of the seven hills,

and cover about one hundred and fifty acres of our own measure.
The seat of Turkish jealousy and despotism is erected on the
foundations of a Grecian republic : but it may be supposed
that the Byzantines were tempted by the conveniency of the
harbour to extend their habitations on that side beyond the
modern limits of the Seraglio. The new walls of Constantine
stretched from the port to the Propontis across the enlarged
breadth of the triangle, at the distance of fifteen stadia from
the ancient fortifications : and with the city of Byzantium they
inclosed five of the seven hills, which to the eyes of those who
approach Constantinople appear to rise above each other in
beautiful order. About a century after the death of the founder
the new buildings, extending on one side up the harbour, and
on the other the Propontis, already covered the narrow ridge of
the sixth and the broad summit of the seventh hill. The
necessity of protecting those suburbs from the incessant inroads
of the barbarians engaged the younger Theodosius to surround
his capital with an adequate and permanent inclosure of walls.
From the eastern promontory to the Golden Gate, the extreme
length of Constantinople was above three Roman miles ; the
circumference measured between ten and eleven ; and the
surface might be computed as equal to about two thousand
English acres. It is impossible to justify the vain and credulous
exaggerations of modern travellers, who have sometimes stretched
the limits of Constantinople over the adjacent villages of the
European and even Asiatic coasts. But the suburbs of Pera
and Galata, though situate beyond the harbour, may deserve to
be considered as a part of the city, and this addition may perhaps
authorise the measure of a Byzantine historian, who assigns sixteen Greek (about sixteen Roman) miles for the circumference of
his native city. Such an extent may seem not unworthy of an
imperial residence. Yet Constantinople must yield to Babylon
and Thebes, to ancient Rome, to London, and even to Paris . . .

" Some estimate may be formed of the expense bestowed with
imperial liberality on Constantinople, by the allowance of about
two millions five hundred thousand pounds for the construction
of the walls, the porticoes, and the aqueducts. The forests that
overshadowed the shores of the Euxine, and the celebrated

I

quarries of white marble in the little island of Proconnesus, supplied an inexhaustible stock of materials ready to be conveyed by the convenience of a short water carriage to the harbour of Byzantium. A multitude of labourers and artificers urged the conclusion of the work with incessant toil, but the impatience of Constantine soon discovered that in the decline of the arts the skill as well as the number of his architects bore a very unequal proportion to the greatness of his design. . . The buildings of the new city were executed by such artificers as the age of Constantine could afford, but they were decorated by the hands of the most celebrated masters of the age of Pericles and Alexander. . . . By Constantine's command the cities of Greece and Asia were despoiled of their most valuable ornaments. The trophies of memorable wars, the objects of religious veneration, the most finished statues of the gods and heroes, of the sages and poets of ancient times, contributed to the splendid triumph of Constantinople.

"· · · · The Circus, or Hippodrome, was a stately building of about four hundred paces in length and one hundred in breadth. The space between the two *metæ*, or gaols, was filled with statues and obelisks, and we may still remark a very singular fragment of antiquity—the bodies of three serpents twisted into one pillar of brass. Their triple heads had once supported the golden tripod which, after the defeat of Xerxes, was consecrated in the temple of Delphi by the victorious Greeks. The beauty of the Hippodrome has been long since defaced by the rude hands of the Turkish conquerors ; but, under the similar appellation of Atmeidan, it still serves as a place of exercise for their horses. From the throne whence the emperor viewed the Circensian games a winding staircase descended to the palace, a magnificent edifice, which scarcely yielded to the residence of Rome itself, and which, together with the dependent courts, gardens, and porticoes, covered a considerable extent of ground upon the banks of the Propontis between the Hippodrome and the church of St. Sophia. We might likewise celebrate the baths, which still retained the name of Zeuxippus, after they had been enriched by the magnificence of Constantine with lofty columns, various marbles, and above three score statues of bronze.

But we should deviate from the design of this history if we attempted minutely to describe the different buildings or quarters of the city. . . . A particular description, composed about a century after its foundation, enumerates a capitol or school of learning, a circus, two theatres, eight public and one hundred and fifty-three private baths, fifty-two porticoes, five granaries, eight aqueducts or reservoirs of water, four spacious halls for the meeting of the senate or courts of justice, fourteen churches, fourteen palaces, and four thousand three hundred and eighty-eight houses, which for their size or beauty deserved to be distinguished from the multitude of plebeian habitations."

Gibbon's conception of history was that of a spacious panorama, in which a series of tableaux pass in succession before the reader's eye. He adverts but little, far too little, to that side of events which does not strike the visual sense. He rarely generalises or sums up a widely-scattered mass of facts into pregnant synthetic views. But possibly he owes some of the permanence of his fame to this very defect. As soon as ever a writer begins to support a thesis, to prove a point, he runs imminent danger of one-sidedness and partiality in his presentation of events. Gibbon's faithful transcript of the past has neither the merit nor the drawback of generalisation, and he has come in consequence to be regarded as a common mine of authentic facts to which all speculators can resort.

The first volume, which was received with such warm acclamation, is inferior to those that followed. He seems to have been partly aware of this himself, and speaks of the "concise and superficial narrative from Commodus to Alexander." But the whole volume lacks the grasp and easy mastery which distinguish its successors. No doubt the subject-matter was comparatively meagre and ungrateful. The century between

Commodus and Diocletian was one long spasm of
anarchy and violence, which was, as Niebuhr said,
incapable of historical treatment. The obscure con-
fusion of the age is aggravated into almost complete
darkness by the wretched materials which alone have
survived, and the attempt to found a dignified narrative
on such scanty and imperfect authorities was hardly
wise. Gibbon would have shown a greater sense of
historic proportion if he had passed over this period
with a few bold strokes, and summed up with brevity
such general results as may be fairly deduced. We may
say of the first volume that it was tentative in every
way. In it the author not only sounded his public, but
he was also trying his instrument, running over the
keys in preparatory search for the right note. He
strikes it full and clear in the two final chapters on the
Early Church; these, whatever objections may be made
against them on other grounds, are the real commencement of the Decline and Fall.

From this point onwards he marches with the steady
and measured tramp of a Roman legion. His materials
improve both in number and quality. The fourth
century, though a period of frightful anarchy and
disaster if compared to a settled epoch, is a period of
relative peace and order when compared to the third
century. The fifth was calamitous beyond example;
but ecclesiastical history comes to the support of
secular history in a way which might have excited more
gratitude in Gibbon than it did. From Constantine to
Augustulus Gibbon is able to put forth all his strength.
His style is less superfine, as his matter becomes more
copious; and the more definite cleavage of events
brought about by the separation between the Eastern

and Western Empires, enables him to display the higher
qualities which marked him as an historian.

The merit of his work, it is again necessary to point
out, will not be justly estimated unless the considerations suggested at the beginning of this chapter be kept
in view. We have to remember that his culture was
chiefly French, and that his opinions were those which
prevailed in France in the latter half of the eighteenth
century. He was the friend of Voltaire, Helvétius, and
D'Holbach ; that is, of men who regarded the past as
one long nightmare of crime, imposture, and folly, insti-
gated by the selfish machinations of kings and priests.
A strong infusion of the spirit which animated not
only Voltaire's *Essay on Manners*, but certain parts of
Hume's *History of England* might have been expected
as a matter of course. It is essentially absent. Gibbon's
private opinions may have been what they will, but he
has approved his high title to the character of an
historian by keeping them well in abeyance. When he
turned his eyes to the past and viewed it with intense
gaze, he was absorbed in the spectacle, his peculiar
prejudices were hushed, he thought only of the object
before him and of reproducing it as well as he could.
This is not the common opinion, but, nevertheless, a
great deal can be said to support it.

It will be as well to take two concrete tests—his
treatment of two topics which of all others were most
likely to betray him into deviations from historic candour.
If he stands these, he may be admitted to stand any less
severe. Let them be his account of Julian, and his
method of dealing with Christianity.

The snare that was spread by Julian's apostasy for the
philosophers of the last century, and their haste to fall

into it, are well known. The spectacle of a philosopher
on the throne who proclaimed toleration, and contempt for
Christianity, was too tempting and too useful controver-
sially to allow of much circumspection in handling it.
The odious comparisons it offered were so exactly what
was wanted for depreciating the Most Christian king and
his courtly Church, that all further inquiry into the
apostate's merits seemed useless. Voltaire finds that
Julian had all the qualities of Trajan without his defects;
all the virtues of Cato without his ill humour; all that
one admires in Julius Cæsar without his vices; he had
the continency of Scipio, and was in all ways equal to
Marcus Aurelius, the first of men. Nay, more. If he
had only lived longer, he would have retarded the fall
of the Roman Empire, if he could not arrest it entirely.
We here see the length to which "polemical fury"
could hurry a man of rare insight. Julian had been a
subject of contention for years between the hostile
factions. While one party made it a point of honour to
prove that he was a monster, warring consciously against
the Most High, the other was equally determined to
prove that he was a paragon of all virtue, by reason of
his enmity to the Christian religion. The deep interest
attaching to the pagan reaction in the fourth century,
and the social and moral problems it suggests, were perceived by neither side, and it is not difficult to see why
they were not. The very word reaction, in its modern
sense, will hardly be found in the eighteenth century,
and the thing that it expresses was very imperfectly
conceived. We, who have been surrounded by reactions,
real or supposed, in politics, in religion, in philosophy,
recognise an old acquaintance in the efforts of the limited,
intense Julian to stem the tide of progress as repre-

sented in the Christian Church. It is a fine instance of
the way in which the ever-unfolding present is constantly lighting up the past. Julian and his party were
the Ultramontanes of their day in matters of religion,
and the Romantics in matters of literature. Those
radical innovators and reformers, the Christians, were
marching from conquest to conquest, over the old faith,
making no concealment of their revolutionary aims and
intentions to wipe out the past as speedily as possible.
The conservatives of those times, after long despising
the reformers, passed easily to fearing them and hating
them as their success became threatening. "The attachment to paganism," says Neander, "lingered especially
in many of the ancient and noble families of Greece and
Rome." Old families, or new rich ones who wished to
be thought old, would be sure to take up the cause of
ancestral wisdom as against modern innovation. Before
Julian came to the throne, a pagan reaction was imminent, as Neander points out. Julian himself was a
remarkable man, as men of his class usually are. In the
breaking up of old modes of belief, as Mill has said,
" the most strong-minded and discerning, next to those
who head the movement, are generally those who bring
up the rear." The energy of his mind and character
was quite exceptional, and if we reflect that he only
reigned sixteen months, and died in his thirty-second
year, we must admit that the mark he has left in history
is very surprising. He and his policy are now discussed
with entire calm by inquirers of all schools, and sincere
Christians like Neander and Dean Milman are as little
disposed to attack him with acrimony, as those of a
different way of thought are inclined to make him a
subject of unlimited panegyric.

Through this difficult subject Gibbon has found his
way with a prudence and true insight which extorted
admiration, even in his own day. His account of
Julian is essentially a modern account. The influence
of his private opinions can hardly be traced in the
brilliant chapters that he has devoted to the Apostate.
He sees through Julian's weaknesses in a way in
which Voltaire never saw or cared to see. His pitiful
superstition, his huge vanity, his weak affectation are
brought out with an incisive clearness and subtle penetration into character which Gibbon was not always so
ready to display. At the same time he does full justice
to Julian's real merits. And this is perhaps the most
striking evidence of his penetration. An error on
the side of injustice to Julian is very natural in a man
who, having renounced allegiance to Christianity, yet
fully realises the futility of attempting to arrest it in
the fourth century. A certain intellectual disdain for
the reactionary emperor is difficult to avoid. Gibbon
surmounts it completely, and he does so, not in consequence of a general conception of the reactionary spirit,
as a constantly emerging element in society, but by sheer
historical insight, clear vision of the fact before him. It
may be added that nowhere is Gibbon's command of
vivid narrative seen to greater advantage than in the
chapters that he has devoted to Julian. The daring
march from Gaul to Illyricum is told with immense
spirit ; but the account of Julian's final campaign and
death in Persia is still better, and can hardly be surpassed. It has every merit of clearness and rapidity,
yet is full of dignity, which culminates in this fine
passage referring to the night before the emperor
received his mortal wound.

" While Julian struggled with the almost insuperable
difficulties of his situation, the silent hours of the night
were still devoted to study and contemplation. Whenever he closed his eyes in short and interrupted slumbers,
his mind was agitated by painful anxiety ; nor can it be
thought surprising that the Genius of the empire should
once more appear before him, covering with a funereal
veil his head and his horn of abundance, and slowly
retiring from the Imperial tent. The monarch started
from his couch, and, stepping forth to refresh his wearied
spirits with the coolness of the midnight air, he beheld
a fiery meteor, which shot athwart the sky and suddenly
vanished. Julian was convinced that he had seen the
menacing countenance of the god of war : the council
which he summoned, of Tuscan Haruspices, unanimously
pronounced that he should abstain from action ; but on
this occasion necessity and reason were more prevalent
than   superstition, and the trumpets sounded at the
break of day." [1]

It will not be so easy to absolve Gibbon from the

---

[1] It is interesting to compare Gibbon's admirable picture with
the harsh original Latin of his authority, Ammianus Marcellinus.
"Ipse autem ad sollicitam suspensamque quietem paullisper pro-
tractus, cum somno (ut solebat) depulso, ad æmulationem Cæsaris
Julii quædam sub pellibus scribens, obscuro noctis altitudine sensus
cujusdam philosophi teneretur, vidit squalidius, ut confessus est
proximis, speciem illam Genii publici, quam quum ad Augustum sur-
geret culmen, conspexit in Galliis, velata cum capite cornucopia per
aulæa tristius discedentem. Et quamquam ad momentum hæsit,
stupore defixus, omni tamen superior metu, ventura decretis cæles-
tibus commendabat ; relicto humi strato cubili, adulta jam excitus
nocte, et numinibus per sacra depulsoria supplicans, flagrantissimam
facem cadenti similem visam, aëris parte sulcata evanuisse existi-
mavit : horroreque perfusus est, ne ita aperte minax Martis ad-
paruerit sidus."—*Amm. Marc.* lib. xxv. cap. 2.

charge of prejudice in reference to his treatment of the
Early Church. It cannot be denied that in the two
famous chapters, at least, which concluded his first
volume, he adopted a tone which must be pronounced
offensive, not only from the Christian point of view, but
on the broad ground of historical equity. His precon-
ceived opinions were too strong for him on this occasion,
and obstructed his generally clear vision. Yet a distinction must be made. The offensive tone in question is
confined to these two chapters. We need not think that
it was in consequence of the clamour they raised that
he adopted a different style with reference to church
matters in his subsequent volumes. A more creditable explanation of his different tone, which will be
presently suggested, is at least as probable. In any
case, these two chapters remain the chief slur on his
historical impartiality, and it is worth while to examine
what his offence amounts to.

Gibbon's account of the early Christians is vitiated by
his narrow and distorted conception of the emotional
side of man's nature. Having no spiritual aspirations
himself, he could not appreciate or understand them in
others. Those emotions which have for their object the
unseen world and its centre, God, had no meaning for
him; and he was tempted to explain them away when
he came across them, or to ascribe their origin and
effects to other instincts which were more intelligible
to him. The wonderland which the mystic inhabits was
closed to him, he remained outside of it and reproduced
in sarcastic travesty the reports he heard of its marvels.
What he has called the secondary causes of the growth
of Christianity, were much rather its effects. The first
is " the inflexible and intolerant zeal of the Christians "

and their abhorrence of idolatry. With great power of
language, he paints the early Christian " encompassed
with infernal snares in every convivial entertainment,
as often as his friends, invoking the hospitable deities,
poured out libations to each other's happiness. When
the bride, struggling with well-affected reluctance, was
forced in hymenæal pomp over the threshold of her new
habitation, or when the sad procession of the dead slowly
moved towards the funeral pile, the Christian on these
interesting occasions was compelled to desert the persons
who were dearest to him, rather than contract the guilt
inherent in those impious ceremonies." It is strange
that Gibbon did not ask himself what was the cause of
this inflexible zeal. The zeal produced the effects alleged,
but what produced the zeal ? He says that it was derived
from the Jewish religion, but neglects to point out what
could have induced Gentiles of every diversity of origin
to derive from a despised race tenets and sentiments
which would make their lives one long scene of self-
denial and danger. The whole vein of remark is so
completely out of date, that it is not worth dwelling on,
except very summarily.

The second cause is " the doctrine of a future life,
improved by every additional circumstance which could
give weight and efficacy to that important truth." Again
we have an effect treated as a cause. " The ancient
Christians were animated by a contempt for their
present existence, and by a just confidence of immortality." Very true; but the fact of their being so
animated was what wanted explaining. Gibbon says it
" was no wonder that so advantageous an offer " as that
of immortality was accepted. Yet he had just before told
us that the ablest orators at the bar and in the senate

of Rome, could expose this offer of immortality to ridicule
without fear of giving offence. Whence arose, then,
the sudden blaze of conviction with which the Christians
embraced it?

The third cause is the miraculous powers *ascribed* to
the primitive Church. Gibbon apparently had not the
courage to admit that he agreed with his friend Hume in
rejecting miracles altogether. He conceals his drift in a
cloud of words, suggesting indirectly with innuendo and
sneer his real opinion. But this does not account for
the stress he lays on the *ascription* of miracles. He seems
to think that the claim of supernatural gifts somehow
had the same efficacy as the gifts themselves would have
had, if they had existed.

The fourth cause is the virtues of the primitive Christians. The paragraphs upon it, Dean Milman considers
the most uncandid in all the history, and they certainly
do Gibbon no credit. With a strange ignorance of the
human heart, he attributes the austere morals of the
early Christians to their care for their reputation. The
ascetic temper, one of the most widely manifested in
history, was beyond his comprehension.

The fifth cause was the union and discipline of the
Christian republic. For the last time the effect figures as
the cause. Union and discipline we know are powerful,
but we know also that they are the result of deep ante-
cedent forces, and that prudence and policy alone never
produced them.

It can surprise no one that Gibbon has treated the
early Church in a way which is highly unsatisfactory if
judged by a modern standard. Not only is it a period
which criticism has gone over again and again with a
microscope, but the standpoint from which such periods

are observed has materially changed since his day. That dim epoch of nascent faith, full of tender and subdued tints, with a high light on the brows of the Crucified, was not one in which he could see clearly, or properly see at all. He has as little insight into the religious condition of the pagan world, as of the Christian. It is singular how he passes over facts which were plain before him, which he knew quite well, as he knew nearly everything connected with his subject, but the real significance of which he missed. Thus he attributes to the scepticism of the pagan world the easy introduction of Christianity. Misled by the "eloquence of Cicero and the wit of Lucian," he supposes the second century to have been vacant of beliefs, in which a "fashion of incredulity" was widely diffused, and "many were almost disengaged from artificial prejudices." He was evidently unaware of the striking religious revival which uplifted paganism in the age of Hadrian, and grew with the sinking empire : the first stirrings of it may even be discerned in Tacitus, and go on increasing till we reach the theurgy of the Neoplatonists. A growing fear of the gods, a weariness of life and longing for death, a disposition to look for compensation for the miseries of this world to a brighter one beyond the grave—these traits are common in the literature of the second century, and show the change which had come over the minds of men. Gibbon is colour blind to these shades of the religious spirit : he can only see the banter of Lucian.[1] In reference

---

[1] On the religious revival of the second century, see Hausrath's *Neutestamentliche Zeitgeschichte*, vol. iii., especially the sections, "Hadrian's Mysticismus" and "Religiöse Tendenzen in Kunst und Literatur," where this interesting subject is handled with a freshness and insight quite remarkable.

to these matters he was a true son of his age, and could
hardly be expected to transcend it.

He cannot be cleared of this reproach. On the other
hand, we must remember that Gibbon's hard and accurate
criticism set a good example in one respect. The fertile
fancy of the middle ages had run into wild exaggerations
of the number of the primitive martyrs, and their legends
had not always been submitted to impartial scrutiny even
in the eighteenth century. We may admit that Gibbon
was not without bias of another kind, and that his tone
is often very offensive when he seeks to depreciate the
evidence of the sufferings of the early confessors. His
computation, which will allow of "an annual consumption
of a hundred and fifty martyrs," is nothing short of
cynical. Still he did good service in insisting on chapter
and verse and fair historical proof of these frightful
stories, before they were admitted. Dean Milman acknowledges so much, and defends him against the hot
zeal of M. Guizot, justly adding that "truth must
not be sacrificed even to well-grounded moral indignation," in which sentiment all now will no doubt be
willing to concur.

The difference between the Church in the Catacombs,
and the Church in the Palaces at Constantinople or
Ravenna, measures the difference between Gibbon's
treatment of early Christian history and his treatment
of ecclesiastical history. Just as the simple-hearted
emotions of God-fearing men were a puzzle and an irri-
tation to him, so he was completely at home in exposing
the intrigues of courtly bishops and in the metaphysics
of theological controversy. His mode of dealing with
Church matters from this point onward is hardly ever
unfair, and has given rise to few protestations. He

has not succeeded in pleasing everybody. What Church historian ever does? But he is candid, impartial, and discerning. His account of the conversion of Constantine is remarkably just, and he is more generous to the first Christian Emperor than Niebuhr or Neander. He plunges into the Arian controversy with manifest delight, and has given in a few pages one of the clearest and most memorable *résumés* of that great struggle. But it is when he comes to the hero of that struggle, to an historic character who can be seen with clearness, that he shows his wonted tact and insight. A great man hardly ever fails to awaken Gibbon into admiration and sympathy. The "Great Athanasius," as he often calls him, caught his eye at once, and the impulse to draw a fine character, promptly silenced any prejudices which might interfere with faithful portraiture. "Athanasius stands out more grandly in Gibbon, than in the pages of the orthodox ecclesiastical historians"—Dr. Newman has said,—a judge whose competence will not be questioned. And as if to show how much insight depends on sympathy, Gibbon is immediately more just and open to the merits of the Christian community, than he had been hitherto. He now sees "that the privileges of the Church had already revived a sense of order and freedom in the Roman government." His chapter on the rise of monasticism is more fair and discriminating than the average Protestant treatment of that subject. He distinctly acknowledges the debt we owe the monks for their attention to agriculture, the useful trades, and the preservation of ancient literature. The more disgusting forms of asceticism he touches with light irony, which is quite as effective as the vehement denunciations of non-Catholic writers. It must not be forgotten that

his ecclesiastical history derives a great superiority of
clearness and proportion by its interweaving with the
general history of the times, and this fact of itself
suffices to give Gibbon's picture a permanent value even
beside the master works of German erudition which
have been devoted exclusively to Church matters. If
we lay down Gibbon and take up Neander, for instance,
we are conscious that with all the greater fulness of
detail, engaging candour, and sympathetic insight of
the great Berlin Professor, the general impression of
the times is less distinct and lasting.   There is no
specialism in Gibbon; his book is a broad sociological
picture in which the whole age is portrayed.

To sum up. In two memorable chapters Gibbon has
allowed his prejudices to mar his work as an historian.
But two chapters out of seventy-one constitute a small
proportion.   In the remainder of his work he is as
free from bias and unfairness as human frailty can
well allow.   The annotated editions of Milman and
Guizot are guarantees of this.   Their critical animad-
versions become very few and far between after the
first volume is passed. If he had been animated by a
polemical object in writing ; if he had used the past as
an arsenal from which to draw weapons to attack the
present, we may depend that a swift blight would have
shrivelled his labours, as it did so many famous works
of the eighteenth century, when the great day of reaction
set in. His mild rebuke of the Abbé Raynal should not
be forgotten. He admired the *History of the Indies*. It is
one of the few books that he has honoured with mention
and praise in the text of his own work. But he points
out that the "zeal of the philosophic historian for the
rights of mankind" had led him into a blunder.   It

was not only Gibbon's scholarly accuracy which saved him from such blunders. Perhaps he had less zeal for the rights of mankind than men like Raynal, whose general views he shared. But it is certain that he did not write with their settled *parti pris* of making history a vehicle of controversy. His object was to be a faithful historian, and due regard being had to his limitations, he attained to it.

If we now consider the defects of the *Decline and Fall*—which the progress of historic study, and still more the lapse of time, have gradually rendered visible, they will be found, as was to be expected, to consist in the author's limited conception of society, and of the multitudinous forces which mould and modify it. We are constantly reminded by the tone of remark that he sees chiefly the surface of events, and that the deeper causes which produce them have not been seen with the same clearness. In proportion as an age is remote, and therefore different from that in which a historian writes, does it behove him to remember that the social and general side of history is more important than the individual and particular. In reference to a period adjacent to our own the fortunes of individuals properly take a prominent place, the social conditions amid which they worked are familiar to us, and we understand them and their position without effort. But with regard to a remote age the case is different. Here our difficulty is to understand the social conditions, so unlike those with which we are acquainted, and as society is greater than man, so we feel that society, and not individual men, should occupy the chief place in the picture. Not that individuals are to be suppressed or neglected, but their subordination to the large

K

historic background must be well maintained. The social,
religious, and philosophic conditions amid which they
played their parts should dominate the scene, and dwarf
by their grandeur and importance the human actors
who move across it.   The higher historical style now
demands what may be called compound narrative, that
is narrative having reference to two sets of phenomena
—one the obvious surface events, the other the larger
and wider, but less obvious, sociological condition. A
better example could hardly be given than Grote's
account of the mutilation of the Hermæ.   The fact
of the mutilation is told in the briefest way in a few
lines, but the social condition which overarched it,
and made the disfiguring of a number of half-statues
" one of the most extraordinary events in Greek history,"
demands five pages of reflections and commentary to
bring out its full significance.   Grote insists on the
duty " to take reasonable pains to realise in our minds
the religious and political associations of the Athenians,"
and helps us to do it by a train of argument and illus-
tration.   The larger part of the strength of the modern
historical school lies in this method, and in able hands
it has produced great results.

It would be unfair to compare Gibbon to these
writers. They had a training in social studies which
he had not.   But it is not certain that he has always
acquitted himself well, even if compared to his contemporaries and predecessors, Montesquieu, Mably, and
Voltaire. In any case his narrative is generally wanting in historic perspective and suggestive background.
It adheres closely to the obvious surface of events with
little attempt to place behind them the deeper sky of
social evolution.   In many of his crowded chapters one

cannot see the wood for the trees. The story is not
lifted up and made lucid by general points of view, but
drags or hurries along in the hollow of events, over
which the author never seems to raise himself into
a position of commanding survey. The thirty-sixth
chapter is a marked instance of this defect. But the
defect is general. The vigorous and skilful narrative,
and a certain grandeur and weightiness of language,
make us overlook it. It is only when we try to
attain clear and succinct views, which condense into
portable propositions the enormous mass of facts collected before us, that we feel that the writer has not
often surveyed his subject from a height and distance
sufficient to allow the great features of the epoch to be
seen in bold outline. By the side of the history of
concrete events, we miss the presentation of those
others which are none the less events for being vague,
irregular, and wide-reaching, and requiring centuries for
their accomplishment. Gibbon's manner of dealing with
the first is always good, and sometimes consummate,
and equal to anything in historical literature. The
thirty-first chapter, with its description of Rome, soon
to fall a prey to the Goths and Alaric, is a masterpiece,
artistic and spacious in the highest degree ; though it is
unnecessary to cite particular instances, as nearly every
chapter contains passages of admirable historic power.
But the noble flood of narrative never stops in medi-
tative pause to review the situation, and point out
with pregnant brevity what is happening in the sum
total, abstraction made of all confusing details. Besides
the facts of the time, we seek to have the tendencies of the
age brought before us in their flow and expansion, the
filiation of events over long periods deduced in clear

sequence, a synoptical view which is to the mind what a
picture is to the eye. In this respect Gibbon's method
leaves not a little to be desired.

Take for instance two of the most important aspects of
the subject that he treated : the barbarian invasions, and
the causes of the decline and fall of the Roman empire.
To the concrete side of both he has done ample justice.
The rational and abstract side of neither has received
the attention from him which it deserved. On the
interesting question of the introduction of the barbarians into the frontier provinces, and their incor-
poration into the legions, he never seems to have quite
made up his mind. In the twelfth chapter he calls it
a "great and beneficial plan." Subsequently he calls it
a disgraceful and fatal expedient. He recurs frequently
to the subject in isolated passages, but never collects
the facts, into a focus, with a view of deducing their real
meaning. Yet the point is second to none in importance. Its elucidation throws more light on the fall of
Rome than any other considerations whatever. The
question is, Whether Rome was conquered by the barbarians in the ordinary sense of the word, conquered.
We know that it was not, and Gibbon knew that it was
not. Yet perhaps most people rise from reading his
book with an impression that the empire succumbed to
the invasion of the barbarians, as Carthage, Gaul, and
Greece had succumbed to the invasion of the Romans ;
that the struggle lay between classic Rome and outside
uncivilised foes ; and that after two centuries of hard
fighting the latter were victorious. The fact that the
struggle lay between barbarians, who were within
and friendly to the empire, and barbarians who were
without it, and hostile rather to their more fortunate

brethren, than to the empire which employed them, is implicitly involved in Gibbon's narrative, but it is not explicitly brought out. Romanised Goths, Vandals, and Franks were the defenders, nearly the only defenders, of the empire against other tribes and nations who were not Romanised, and nothing can be more plain than that Gibbon saw this as well as any one since, but he has not set it forth with prominence and clearness. With his complete mastery of the subject he would have done it admirably, if he had assumed the necessary point of view.

Similarly, with regard to the causes of the fall of the empire. It is quite evident that he was not at all unconscious of the deep economic and social vices which undermined the great fabric. Depopulation, decay of agriculture, fiscal oppression, the general prostration begotten of despotism—all these sources of the great collapse may be traced in his text, or his wonderful notes, hinted very often with a flashing insight which anticipates the most recent inquiries into the subject. But these considerations are not brought together to a luminous point, nor made to yield clear and tangible results. They lie scattered, isolated, and barren over three volumes, and are easily overlooked. One may say that generalised and synthetic views are conspicuous by their absence in Gibbon.

But what of that? These reflections, even if they be well founded, hardly dim the majesty of the *Decline and Fall*. The book is such a marvel of knowledge at once wide and minute, that even now, after numbers of labourers have gone over the same ground, with only special objects in view, small segments of the great circle which Gibbon fills alone, his word is still one of

the weightiest that can be quoted. Modern research
has unquestionably opened out points of view to which
he did not attain.   But when it comes to close investigation of any particular question, we rarely fail to find
that he has seen it, dropped some pregnant hint about
it, more valuable than the dissertations of other men.
As Mr. Freeman says, " Whatever else is read, Gibbon
must be read too."

CHAPTER VIII.

AFTER the preliminary troubles which met him on his
arrival at Lausanne, Gibbon had four years of unbroken
calm and steady work, of which there is nothing to
record beyond the fact that they were filled with peaceful industry. " One day," he wrote, " glides by another
in tranquil uniformity." During the whole period he
never stirred ten miles out of Lausanne. He had nearly
completed the fourth volume before he left England.
Then came an interruption of a year—consumed in the
break-up of his London establishment, his journey, the
transport of his library, the delay in getting settled at
Lausanne. Then he sat down in grim earnest to finish
his task, and certainly the speed he used, considering
the quality of the work, left nothing to be desired. He
achieved the fifth volume in twenty-one months, and the
sixth in little more than a year. He had hoped to
finish sooner, but it is no wonder that he found his
work grow under his hands when he passed from design
to execution. " A long while ago, when I contemplated
the distant prospect of my work," he writes to Lord
Sheffield, " I gave you and myself some hopes of landing

in England last autumn ; but alas ! when autumn grew
near, hills began to rise on hills, Alps on Alps, and I
found my journey far more tedious and toilsome than I
had imagined. When I look back on the length of the
undertaking and the variety of materials, I cannot
accuse or suffer myself to be accused of idleness ; yet it
appeared that unless I doubled my diligence, another
year, and perhaps more, would elapse before I could
embark with my complete manuscript. Under these
circumstances I took, and am still executing, a bold and
meritorious resolution. The mornings in winter, and in
a country of early dinners, are very concise. To them,
my usual period of study, I now frequently add the
evenings, renounce cards and society, refuse the most
agreeable evenings, or perhaps make my appearance at
a late supper. By this extraordinary industry, which I
never practised before, and to which I hope never to
be again reduced, I see the last part of my history
growing apace under my hands." He was indeed, as he
said, now straining for the goal which was at last
reached "on the day, or rather the night, of the 27th of
June, 1787. Between the hours of eleven and twelve
I wrote the last lines of the last page in a summer-
house in my garden. After laying down my pen, I took
several turns in a berceau, or covered walk of acacias,
which commands a prospect of the country, the lake, and
the mountains. The air was temperate, the sky was
serene, the silver orb of the moon was reflected from the
waters, and all nature was silent. I will not dissemble
the first emotions of joy on the recovery of my freedom,
and perhaps the establishment of my fame. But my
pride was soon humbled, and a sober melancholy was
spread over my mind by the idea that I had taken an

everlasting leave of an old and agreeable companion, and
that whatsoever might be the future fate of my history,
the life of the historian must be short and precarious."

A faint streak of poetry occasionally shoots across
Gibbon's prose. But both prose and poetry had now to
yield to stern business. The printing of three quarto
volumes in those days of handpresses was a formidable
undertaking, and unless expedition were used the
publishing season of the ensuing year would be lost.
A month had barely elapsed before Gibbon with his
precious cargo started for England. He went straight
to his printers. The printing of the fourth volume
occupied three months, and both author and publisher
were warned that their common interest required a
quicker pace. Then Mr. Strahan "fulfilled his engage-
ment, which few printers could sustain, of delivering every
week three thousand copies of nine sheets." On the
8th of May, 1788, the three concluding volumes were
published, and Gibbon had discharged his debt for the
entertainment that he had had in this world.

He returned as speedily as he could to Lausanne, to
rest from his labours. But he had a painful greeting in
the sadly altered look of his friend Deyverdun. Soon
an apoplectic seizure confirmed his forebodings, and
within a twelvemonth the friend of his youth, whom
he had loved for thirty-three years, was taken away
by death (July 4, 1789).[1]

---

[1] The letter in which Gibbon communicated the sad news to
Lord Sheffield was written on the 14th July, 1789, the day of the
taking of the Bastille. So "that evening sun of July" sent its
beams on Gibbon mourning the dead friend, as well as on "reapers
amid peaceful woods and fields, on old women spinning in cottages,
on ships far out on the silent main, on balls at the Orangerie of

Gibbon never got over this loss. His staid and solid
nature was not given to transports of joy or grief.
But his constant references to "poor Deyverdun," and
the vacancy caused by his loss, show the depth of the
wound. "I want to change the scene," he writes, "and,
beautiful as the garden and prospect must appear to
every eye, I feel that the state of my mind casts a gloom
over them : every spot, every walk, every bench recalls
the memory of those hours, those conversations, which
will return no more. . . . I almost hesitate whether I shall
run over to England to consult with you on the spot,
and to fly from poor Deyverdun's shade, which meets
me at every turn." Not that he lacked attached
friends, and of mere society and acquaintance he had
more than abundance. He occupied at Lausanne a
position of almost patriarchal dignity, "and may be
said," writes Lord Sheffield, "to have almost given the
law to a set of as willing subjects as any man ever
presided over." Soon the troubles in France sent
wave after wave of emigrants over the frontiers, and
Lausanne had its full share of the exiles. After a brief
approval of the reforms in France he passed rapidly to
doubt, disgust, and horror at the "new birth of time"
there. "You will allow me to be a tolerable historian,"
he wrote to his stepmother, "yet on a fair review of
ancient and modern times I can find none that bear
any affinity to the present." The last social evolution
was beyond his power of classification. The mingled
bewilderment and anger with which he looks out from
Lausanne on the revolutionary welter, form an almost
amusing contrast to his usual apathy on political matters.

Versailles, where high-rouged dames of the palace are even now
dancing with double-jacketed Hussar officers."

He is full of alarm lest England should catch the revolutionary fever. He is delighted with Burke's *Reflections*. "I admire his eloquence, I approve his politics,
I adore his chivalry, and I can forgive even his
superstition." His wrath waxes hotter at every post.
"Poor France! The state is dissolved! the nation is
mad." At last nothing but vituperation can express his
feelings, and he roundly calls the members of the Con-
vention "devils," and discovers that "democratical principles lead by a path of flowers into the abyss of hell."

In 1790 his friends the Neckers had fled to Switzerland, and on every ground of duty and inclination he was
called upon to show them the warmest welcome, and he
did so in a way that excited their liveliest gratitude.
Necker was cast down in utter despair, not only for the
loss of place and power, but on account of the strong
animosity which was shown to him by the exiled French,
none of whom would set their foot in his house. The
Neckers were now Gibbon's chief intimates till the end
of his sojourn in Switzerland. They lived at Coppet, and
constant visits were exchanged there and at Lausanne.
Madame Necker wrote to him frequent letters, which
prove that if she had ever had any grievance to complain of in the past, it was not only forgiven, but entirely forgotten. The letters, indeed, testify a warmth
of sentiment on her part which, coming from a lady of
less spotless propriety, would almost imply a revival of
youthful affection for her early lover. "You have
always been dear to me," she writes, "but the friendship you have shown to M. Necker adds to that which
you inspire me with on so many grounds, and I love
you at present with a double affection."—"Come to us
when you are restored to health and to yourself; that

moment should always belong to your first and your
last friend (*amie*), and I do not know which of those
titles is the sweetest and dearest to my heart."—
" Near you, the recollections you recalled were pleasant
to me, and you connected them easily with present
impressions ; the chain of years seemed to link all
times together with electrical rapidity ; you were at
once twenty and fifty years old for me. Away from
you the different places, which I have inhabited are only
the milestones of my life telling me of the distance
I have come." With much more in the same strain.
Of Madame de Stael Gibbon does not speak in very
warm praise. Her mother, who was far from being
contented with her, may perhaps have prejudiced him
against her. In one letter to him she complains of her
daughter's conduct in no measured terms. Yet Gibbon
owns that Madame de Staël was a "pleasant little
woman ; " and in another place says that she was " wild,
vain, but good-natured, with a much larger provision of
wit than of beauty." One wonders if he ever knew of
her childish scheme of marrying him in order that her
parents might always have the pleasure of his company
and conversation.

These closing years of Gibbon's life were not happy,
through no fault of his. No man was less inclined by
disposition to look at the dark side of things. But
heavy blows fell on him in quick succession. His
health was seriously impaired, and he was often laid up
for months with the gout. His neglect of exercise had
produced its effect, and he had become a prodigy of
unwieldy corpulency. Unfortunately his digestion
seems to have continued only too good, and neither his
own observation nor the medical science of that day

sufficed to warn him against certain errors of regimen
which were really fatal. All this time, while the gout
was constantly torturing him, he drank Madeira freely.
There is frequent question of a pipe of that sweet wine
in his correspondence with Lord Sheffield. He cannot
bear the thought of being without a sufficient supply, as
" good Madeira is now become essential to his health and
reputation." The last three years of his residence at
Lausanne were agitated by perpetual anxiety and dread
of an invasion of French democratic principles, or even
of French troops. Reluctance to quit "his paradise"
keeps him still, but he is always wondering how soon
he will have to fly, and often regrets that he has not
done so already. "For my part," he writes, "till
Geneva falls, I do not think of a retreat; but at all
events I am provided with two strong horses and a
hundred louis in gold." Fate was hard on the kindly
epicurean, who after his long toil had made his bed in
the sun, on which he was preparing to lie down in genial
content till the end came. But he feels he must not
think of rest; and that, heavy as he is, and irksome to
him as it is to move, he must before long be a rover
again. Still he is never peevish upon his fortune; he
puts the best face on things as long as they will
bear it.

He was not so philosophical under the bereavements
that he now suffered. His aunt, Mrs. Porten, had died
in 1786. He deplored her as he was bound to do, and
feelingly regrets and blames himself for not having
written to her as often as he might have done since their
last parting. Then came the irreparable loss of Deyverdun. Shortly, an old Lausanne friend, M. de Severy,
to whom he was much attached, died after a long illness.

Lastly and suddenly, came the death of Lady Sheffield,
the wife of his friend Holroyd, with whom he had long
lived on such intimate terms that he was in the habit of
calling her his sister. The Sheffields, father and mother
and two daughters, had spent the summer of 1791 with
him at Lausanne. The visit was evidently an occasion
of real happiness and *épanchement de cœur* to the two
old friends, and supplied Gibbon for nearly two years
with tender regrets and recollections. Then, without
any warning, he heard of Lady Sheffield's death. In
a moment his mind was made up : he would go at once
to console his friend. All the fatigue and irksomeness
of the journey to one so ailing and feeble, all the dangers
of the road lined and perhaps barred by hostile armies,
vanished on the spot. Within twelve days he had
made his preparations and started on his journey.
He was forced to travel through Germany, and in his
ignorance of the language he required an interpreter ;
young de Severy, the son of his deceased friend,
joyfully, and out of mere affection for him, undertook
the office of courier. "His attachment to me," wrote
Gibbon, "is the sole motive which prompts him to undertake this troublesome journey." It is clear that
he had the art of making himself loved. He travelled
through Frankfort, Cologne, Brussels, Ostend, and was
by his friend's side in little more than a month after
he had received the fatal tidings. Well might Lord
Sheffield say, "I must ever regard it as the most enduring proof of his sensibility, and of his possessing the
true spirit of friendship, that, after having relinquished
the thought of his intended visit, he hastened to England,
in spite of increasing impediments, to soothe me by the
most generous sympathy, and to alleviate my domestic

affliction; neither his great corpulency nor his extraordinary bodily infirmities, nor any other consideration,
could prevent him a moment from resolving on an
undertaking that might have deterred the most active
young man. He almost immediately, with an alertness
by no means natural to him, undertook a great circuitous
journey along the frontier of an enemy worse than savage,
within the sound of their cannon, within the range of the
light troops of the different armies, and through roads
ruined by the enormous machinery of war.''

In this public and private gloom he bade for ever
farewell to Lausanne. He was himself rapidly approaching

> " The dark portal,
> Goal of all mortal,"

but of this he knew not as yet. While he is in the
house of mourning, beside his bereaved friend, we will
return for a short space to consider the conclusion of
his great work.

CHAPTER IX.

THE thousand years between the fifth and the fifteenth century comprise the middle age, a period which only recently, through utterly inadequate conceptions of social growth, was wont to be called the dark ages. That long epoch of travail and growth, during which the old field of civilisation was broken up and sown afresh with new and various seed unknown to antiquity, receives now on all hands due recognition, as being one of the most rich, fertile, and interesting in the history of man. The all-embracing despotism of Rome was replaced by the endless local divisions and subdivisions of feudal tenure. The multiform rites and beliefs of polytheism were replaced by the single faith and paramount authority of the Catholic Church. The philosophies of Greece were dethroned, and the scholastic theology reigned in their stead. The classic tongues crumbled away, and out of their *débris* arose the modern idioms of France, Italy, and Spain, to which were added in Northern Europe the new forms of Teutonic speech. The fine and useful arts took a new departure ; slavery was mitigated into serfdom ; industry and commerce became powers in the world as they had never been

before ; the narrow municipal polity of the old world
was in time succeeded by the broader national institutions based on various forms of representation. Gunpowder, America, and the art of printing were discovered, and the most civilised portion of mankind
passed insensibly into the modern era.

Such was the wide expanse which spread out before
Gibbon when he resolved to continue his work from the
fall of the Western Empire to the capture of Constantinople. Indeed his glance took in a still wider field, as
he was concerned as much with the decay of Eastern
as of Western Rome, and the long-retarded fall of the
former demanded large attention to the Oriental popu-
lations who assaulted the city and remaining empire of
Constantine. So bold an historic enterprise was never
conceived as when, standing on the limit of antiquity in
the fifth century, he determined to pursue in rapid but
not hasty survey the great lines of events for a thousand
years, to follow in detail the really great transactions
while discarding the less important, thereby giving
prominence and clearness to what is memorable, and
reproducing on a small scale the flow of time through
the ages. It is to this portion of Gibbon's work that
the happy comparison has been made, that it resembles
a magnificent Roman aqueduct spanning over the chasm
which separates the ancient from the modern world. In
these latter volumes he frees himself from the trammels
of regular annalistic narrative, deals with events in
broad masses according to their importance, expanding
or contracting his story as occasion requires ; now
painting in large panoramic view the events of a few
years, now compressing centuries into brief outline.
Many of his massive chapters afford materials for

L

volumes, and are well worthy of a fuller treatment than
he could give without deranging his plan. But works
of greater detail and narrower compass can never compete with Gibbon's history, any more than a county map
can compete with a map of England or of Europe.

The variety of the contents of these last three
volumes is amazing, especially when the thoroughness
and perfection of the workmanship are considered.
Prolix compilations or sketchy outlines of universal history have their use and place, but they are removed by
many degrees from the *Decline and Fall,* or rather they
belong to another species of authorship. It is not only
that Gibbon combines width and depth, that the extent
of his learning is as wonderful as its accuracy, though
in this respect he has hardly a full rival in literature.
The quality which places him not only in the first rank
of historians, but in a class by himself, and makes him
greater than the greatest, lies in his supreme power of
moulding into lucid and coherent unity, the manifold
and rebellious mass of his multitudinous materials, of
coercing his divergent topics into such order that they
seem spontaneously to grow like branches out of one
stem, clear and visible to the mind. There is something
truly epic in these latter volumes. Tribes, nations, and
empires are the characters; one after another they
come forth like Homeric heroes, and do their mighty
deeds before the assembled armies. The grand and
lofty chapters on Justinian; on the Arabs; on the
Crusades, have a rounded completeness, coupled with
such artistic subordination to the main action, that they
read more like cantos of a great prose poem than the
ordinary staple of historical composition. It may well
be questioned whether there is another instance of such

high literary form and finish, coupled with such vast erudition. And two considerations have to be borne in mind, which heighten Gibbon's merit in this respect. (1.) Almost the whole of his subject had been as yet untouched by any preceding writer of eminence, and he had no stimulus or example from his precursors. He united thus in himself the two characters of pioneer and artist. (2.) The barbarous and imperfect nature of the materials with which he chiefly had to work,—dull inferior writers, whose debased style was their least defect.   A historian who has for his authorities masters of reason and language such as Herodotus, Thucydides, Livy, and Tacitus is borne up by their genius; apt quotation and translation alone suffice to produce considerable effects; or in the case of subjects taken from modern times, weighty state papers, eloquent debates, or finished memoirs supply ample materials for graphic narrative.   But Gibbon had little but dross to deal with.   Yet he has smelted and cast it into the grand shapes we see.

The fourth volume is nearly confined to the reign, or rather epoch, of Justinian,—a magnificent subject, which he has painted in his loftiest style of gorgeous narrative. The campaigns of Belisarius and Narses are related with a clearness and vigour that make us feel that Gibbon's merits as a military historian have not been quite sufficiently recognised.   He had from the time of his service in the militia taken continued interest in tactics and all that was connected with the military art.   It was no idle boast when he said that the captain of the Hampshire grenadiers had not been useless to the historian of the Roman empire.   Military matters perhaps occupy a somewhat excessive space in his pages.

Still, if the operations of war are to be related, it is
highly important that they should be treated with
intelligence, and knowledge how masses of men are
moved, and by a writer to whom the various incidents
of the camp, the march, and the bivouac, are not
matters of mere hearsay, but of personal experience.
The campaign of Belisarius in Africa may be quoted
as an example.

"In the seventh year of the reign of Justinian, and about the
time of the summer solstice, the whole fleet of six hundred
ships was ranged in martial pomp before the gardens of the
palace. The patriarch pronounced his benediction, the emperor
signified his last commands, the general's trumpet gave the
signal of departure, and every heart, according to its fears or
wishes, explored with anxious curiosity the omens of misfortune
or success. The first halt was made at Perintheus, or Heraclea,
where Belisarius waited five days to receive some Thracian
horses, a military gift of his sovereign. From thence the fleet
pursued their course through the midst of the Propontis; but
as they struggled to pass the straits of the Hellespont, an
unfavourable wind detained them four days at Abydos, where
the general exhibited a remarkable lesson of firmness and
severity. Two of the Huns who, in a drunken quarrel, had
slain one of their fellow-soldiers, were instantly shown to the
army suspended on a lofty gibbet. The national dignity was
resented by their countrymen, who disclaimed the servile laws
of the empire and asserted the free privileges of Scythia, where
a small fine was allowed to expiate the sallies of intemperance
and anger. Their complaints were specious, their clamours
were loud, and the Romans were not averse to the example of
disorder and impunity. But the rising sedition was appeased
by the authority and eloquence of the general, and he represented to the assembled troops the obligation of justice, the
importance of discipline, the rewards of piety and virtue, and
the unpardonable guilt of murder, which, in his apprehension,
was aggravated rather than excused by the vice of intoxication.

In the navigation from the Hellespont to the Peloponnesus, which the Greeks after the siege of Troy had performed in four days, the fleet of Belisarius was guided in their course by his master-galley, conspicuous in the day by the redness of the sails, and in the night by torches blazing from the masthead. It was the duty of the pilots as they steered between the islands and turned the capes of Malea and Tænarium to preserve the just order and regular intervals of such a multitude. As the wind was fair and moderate, their labours were not unsuccessful, and the troops were safely disembarked at Methone, on the Messenian coast, to repose themselves for a while after the fatigues of the sea. . . . . From the port of Methone the pilots steered along the western coast of Peloponnesus, as far as the island of Zacynthus, or Zante, before they undertook the voyage (in their eyes a most arduous voyage) of one hundred leagues over the Ionian sea. As the fleet was surprised by a calm, sixteen days were consumed in the slow navigation. . . At length the harbour of Caucana, on the southern side of Sicily, afforded a secure and hospitable shelter. . . Belisarius determined to hasten his operations, and his wise impatience was seconded by the winds. The fleet lost sight of Sicily, passed before the island of Malta, discovered the capes of Africa, ran along the coast with a strong gale from the north-east, and finally cast anchor at the promontory of Caput Vada, about five days journey to the south of Carthage. . . . .

" Three months after their departure from Constantinople, the men and the horses, the arms and the military stores were safely disembarked, and five soldiers were left as a guard on each of the ships, which were disposed in the form of a semicircle. The remainder of the troops occupied a camp on the seashore, which they fortified, according to ancient discipline, with a ditch and rampart, and the discovery of a source of fresh water, while it allayed the thirst, excited the superstitious confidence of the Romans. . . The small town of Sullecte, one day's journey from the camp, had the honour of being foremost to open her gates and resume her ancient allegiance ; the larger cities of Leptis and Adrumetum imitated the example of loyalty as soon as Belisarius appeared, and he advanced without opposition as far as Grasse, a palace of the Vandal kings, at the distance of fifty miles from Carthage. The weary Romans indulged themselves in the refreshment of shady groves, cool fountains, and delicious fruits. . . In three generations prosperity and a warm climate had dissolved the hardy virtue of the Vandals, who insensibly became the most luxurious of mankind. In their villas and gardens, which might deserve the Persian name of Paradise, they enjoyed a cool and elegant repose, and after the daily use of the bath, the barbarians were seated at a table profusely spread with the delicacies of the land and sea. Their silken robes, loosely flowing after the fashion of the Medes, were embroidered with gold, love and hunting were the labours of their life, and their vacant hours were amused by pantomimes, chariot-races, and the music and dances of the theatre.

"In a march of twelve days the vigilance of Belisarius was constantly awake and active against his unseen enemies, by whom in every place and at every hour he might be suddenly attacked. An officer of confidence and merit, John the Armenian, led the vanguard of three hundred horse. Six hundred Massagetæ covered at a certain distance the left flank, and the whole fleet, steering along the coast, seldom lost sight of the army, which moved each day about twelve miles, and lodged in the evening in strong camps or in friendly towns. The near approach of the Romans to Carthage filled the mind of Gelimer with anxiety and terror. . . . .

"Yet the authority and promises of Gelimer collected a formidable army, and his plans were concerted with some degree of military skill. An order was despatched to his brother Ammatas to collect all the forces of Carthage, and to encounter the van of the Roman army at the distance of ten miles from the city : his nephew Gibamund with two thousand horse was destined to attack their left, when the monarch himself, who silently followed, should charge their rear in a situation which excluded them from the aid and even the view of their fleet. But the rashness of Ammatas was fatal to himself and his country. He anticipated the hour of attack, outstripped his

tardy followers, and was pierced with a mortal wound, after he
had slain with his own hand twelve of his boldest antagonists.
His Vandals fled to Carthage : the highway, almost ten miles,
was strewed with dead bodies, and it seemed incredible that
such multitudes could be slaughtered by the swords of three
hundred Romans. The nephew of Gelimer was defeated after
a slight combat by the six hundred Massagetæ ; they did not
equal the third part of his numbers, but each Scythian was
fired by the example of his chief, who gloriously exercised the
privilege of his family by riding foremost and alone to shoot the
first arrow against the enemy. In the meantime Gelimer himself, ignorant of the event, and misguided by the windings of
the hills, inadvertently passed the Roman army and reached
the scene of action where Ammatas had fallen. He wept the
fate of his brother and of Carthage, charged with irresistible
fury the advancing squadrons, and might have pursued and
perhaps decided the victory, if he had not wasted those
inestimable moments in the discharge of a vain though pious
duty to the dead. While his spirit was broken by this mournful
office, he heard the trumpet of Belisarius, who, leaving Antonina
and his infantry in the camp, pressed forward with his guards
and the remainder of the cavalry to rally his flying troops, and
to restore the fortune of the day. Much room could not be
found in this disorderly battle for the talents of a general ; but
the king fled before the hero, and the Vandals, accustomed only
to a Moorish enemy, were incapable of withstanding the arms
and the discipline of the Romans. . . . . . .
    " As soon as the tumult had subsided, the several parts of the
army informed each other of the accidents of the day, and Belisarius pitched his camp on the field of victory, to which the tenth
milestone from Carthage had applied the Latin appellation of
Decimus. From a wise suspicion of the stratagems and resources
of the Vandals, he marched the next day in the order of battle ;
halted in the evening before the gates of Carthage, and allowed
a night of repose, that he might not, in darkness and disorder,
expose the city to the licence of the soldiers, or the soldiers
themselves to the secret ambush of the city. But as the fears
of Belisarius were the result of calm and intrepid reason, he

was soon satisfied that he might confide without danger in the peaceful and friendly aspect of the capital. Carthage blazed with innumerable torches, the signal of the public joy; the chain was removed that guarded the entrance of the port, the gates were thrown open, and the people with acclamations of gratitude hailed and invited their Roman deliverers. The defeat of the Vandals and the freedom of Africa were announced to the city on the eve of St. Cyprian, when the churches were already adorned and illuminated for the festival of the martyr whom three centuries of superstition had almost raised to a local deity. . . One awful hour reversed the fortunes of the contending parties. The suppliant Vandals, who had so lately indulged the vices of conquerors, sought an humble refuge in the sanctuary of the church; while the merchants of the east were delivered from the deepest dungeon of the palace by their affrighted keeper, who implored the protection of his captives, and showed them through an aperture in the wall the sails of the Roman fleet. After their separation from the army, the naval commanders had proceeded with slow caution along the coast, till they reached the Hermæan promontory, and obtained the first intelligence of the victory of Belisarius. Faithful to his instructions, they would have cast anchor about twenty miles from Carthage, if the more skilful had not represented the perils of the shore and the signs of an impending tempest. Still ignorant of the revolution, they declined however the rash attempt of forcing the chain of the port, and the adjacent harbour and suburb of Mandracium were insulted only by the rapine of a private officer, who disobeyed and deserted his leaders. But the imperial fleet, advancing with a fair wind, steered through the narrow entrance of the Goletta and occupied the deep and capacious lake of Tunis, a secure station about five miles from the capital. No sooner was Belisarius informed of the arrival than he despatched orders that the greatest part of the mariners should be immediately landed to join the triumph and to swell the apparent numbers of the Romans. Before he allowed them to enter the gates of Carthage he exhorted them, in a discourse worthy of himself and the occasion, not to disgrace the glory of their arms, and to remember that the Vandals had been the tyrants, but that *they* were the deliverers of the Africans, who must now be respected as the voluntary and affectionate subjects of their common sovereign. The Romans marched through the street in close ranks, prepared for battle if an enemy had appeared ; the strict order maintained by their general imprinted on their minds the duty of obedience ; and in an age in which custom and impunity almost sanctified the abuse of conquest, the genius of one man repressed the passions of a victorious army. The voice of menace and complaint was silent, the trade of Carthage was not interrupted ; while Africa changed her master and her government, the shops continued open and busy ; and the soldiers, after sufficient guards had been posted, modestly departed to the houses which had been allotted for their reception. Belisarius fixed his residence in the palace, seated himself on the throne of Genseric, accepted and distributed the barbaric spoil, granted their lives to the suppliant Vandals, and laboured to restore the damage which the suburb of Mandracium had sustained in the preceding night. At supper he entertained his principal officers with the form and magnificence of a royal banquet. The victor was respectfully served by the captive officers of the household, and in the moments of festivity, when the impartial spectators applauded the fortune and merit of Belisarius, his envious flatterers secretly shed their venom on every word and gesture which might alarm the suspicions of a jealous monarch. One day was given to these pompous scenes, which may not be despised as useless if they attracted the popular veneration ; but the active mind of Belisarius, which in the pride of victory could suppose defeat, had already resolved that the Roman empire in Africa should not depend on the chance of arms or the favour of the people. The fortifications of Carthage had alone been excepted from the general proscription ; but in the reign of ninety-five years they were suffered to decay by the thoughtless and indolent Vandals. A wiser conqueror restored with incredible despatch the walls and ditches of the city. His liberality encouraged the workmen ; the soldiers, the mariners, and the citizens vied with each other in the salutary labour ; and Gelimer, who had feared to trust his person in an open town, beheld with astonishment and despair the rising strength of an impregnable fortress.

But we have hardly finished admiring the brilliant picture of the conquest of Africa and Italy, before Gibbon gives us further proofs of his many-sided culture and catholicity of mind. His famous chapter on the Roman law has been accepted by the most fastidious experts of an esoteric science as a masterpiece of knowledge, condensation, and lucidity. It has actually been received as a textbook in some of the continental universities, published separately with notes and illustrations. When we consider the neglect of Roman jurisprudence in England till quite recent times, and its severe study on the Continent, we shall better appreciate the mental grasp and vigour which enabled an unprofessional Englishman in the last century to produce such a dissertation. A little further on (chapter forty-seven) the history of the doctrine of the Incarnation, and the controversies that sprang up around it, are discussed with a subtlety worthy of a scientific theologian. It is perhaps the first attempt towards a philosophical history of dogma, less patient and minute than the works of the specialists of modern Germany on the same subject, but for spirit, clearness, and breadth it is superior to those profound but somewhat barbarous writers. The flexibility of intellect which can do justice in quick succession to such diverse subjects is very extraordinary, and assuredly implies great width of sympathy and large receptivity of nature.

Having terminated the period of Justinian, Gibbon makes a halt, and surveys the varied and immense scene through which he will presently pass in many directions. He rapidly discovers *ten* main lines, along which he will advance in succession to his final goal, the conquest of Constantinople. The two pages at the commencement of the forty-eighth chapter, in which he sketches out the remainder of his plan and indicates the topics which he means to treat, are admirable as a luminous *précis*, and for the powerful grasp which they show of his immense subject. It lay spread out all before him, visible in every part to his penetrating eye, and he seems to rejoice in his conscious strength and ability to undertake the historical conquest on which he is about to set out. " Nor will this scope of narrative," he says, " the riches and variety of these materials, be incompatible with the unity of design and composition. As in his daily prayers the Mussulman of Fez or Delhi still turns his face towards the temple of Mecca, the historian's eye will always be fixed on the city of Constantinople." Then follows the catalogue of nations and empires whose fortunes he means to sing. A grander vision, a more majestic procession, never swept before the mind's eye of poet or historian.

And the practical execution is worthy of the initial inspiration. After a rapid and condensed narrative of Byzantine history till the end of the twelfth century, he takes up the brilliant theme of Mahomet and his successors. A few pages on the climate and physical features of Arabia fittingly introduce the subject. And it may be noted in passing that Gibbon's attention to geography, and his skill and taste for geographical description, are remarkable among his many gifts. He was as diligent a student of maps and travels as of historical records, and seems to have had a rare faculty of realising in imagination scenes and countries of which he had only read. In three chapters, glowing with oriental

colour and rapid as a charge of Arab horse, he tells the
story of the prophet and the Saracen empire. Then the
Bulgarians, Hungarians, and Russians appear on the
scene, to be soon followed by the Normans, and their
short but brilliant dominion in Southern Italy. But
now the Seljukian Turks are emerging from the depths
of Asia, taking the place of the degenerate Saracens, in-
vading the Eastern empire and conquering Jerusalem.
The two waves of hostile fanaticism soon meet in the
Crusades.   The piratical seizure of Constantinople by
the Latins brings in view the French and Venetians, the
family of Courtenay and its pleasant digression.   Then
comes the slow agony of the restored Greek empire.
Threatened by the Moguls, it is invaded and dismembered
by the Ottoman Turks.   Constantinople seems ready to
fall into their hands. But the timely diversion of Tamer-
lane produces a respite of half a century.   Nothing
can be more artistic than Gibbon's management of his
subject as he approaches its termination.   He, who is
such a master of swift narrative, at this point introduces
artful pauses, *suspensions* of the final catastrophe, which
heighten our interest in the fate which is hanging over
the city of Constantine.   In 1425 the victorious Turks
have conquered all the Greek empire save the capital.
Amurath II. besieged it for two months, and was only
prevented from taking it by a domestic revolt in Asia
Minor. At the end of his sixty-fifth chapter Gibbon leaves
Constantinople hanging on the brink of destruction, and
paints in glowing colours the military virtues of its
deadly enemies, the Ottomans.   Then he interposes one
of his most finished chapters, of miscellaneous contents,
but terminating in the grand and impressive pages on
the revival of learning in Italy.   There we read of the

"curiosity and emulation of the Latins," of the zeal of Petrarch and the success of Boccace in Greek studies, of Leontius, Pilatus, Bessarion, and Lascaris. A glow of sober enthusiasm warms the great scholar as he paints the early light of that happy dawn. He admits that the "arms of the Turks pressed the flight of the Muses" from Greece to Italy. But he "trembles at the thought that Greece might have been overwhelmed with her schools and libraries, before Europe had emerged from the deluge of barbarism, and that the seeds of science might have been scattered on the winds, before the Italian soil was prepared for their cultivation." In one of the most perfect sentences to be found in English prose he thus describes the Greek tongue : "In their lowest depths of servitude and depression, the subjects of the Byzantine throne were still possessed of a golden key that could unlock the treasures of antiquity, of a musical and prolific language that gives a soul to the objects of sense and a body to the abstractions of philosophy." Meanwhile we are made to feel that the subjects of the Byzantine throne, with their musical speech, that Constantinople with her libraries and schools, will all soon fall a prey to the ravening and barbarous Turk. This brightening light of the Western sky contending with the baleful gloom which is settling down over the East, is one of the most happy contrasts in historical literature. Then comes the end, the preparations and skill of the savage invader, the futile but heroic defence, the overwhelming ruin which struck down the Cross and erected the Crescent over the city of Constantine the Great.

It is one of the many proofs of Gibbon's artistic instinct that he did not end with this great catastrophe.

On the contrary, he adds three more chapters. His fine tact warned him that the tumult and thunder of the final ruin must not be the last sounds to strike the ear. A resolution of the discord was needed; a soft chorale should follow the din and lead to a mellow *adagio* close. And this he does with supreme skill. With ill-suppressed disgust, he turns from New to Old Rome. "Constantinople no longer appertains to the Roman historian—nor shall I enumerate the civil and religious edifices that were profaned or erected by its Turkish masters." Amid the decayed temples and mutilated beauty of the Eternal City, he moves down to a melodious and pathetic conclusion—piously visits the remaining fragments of ancient splendour and art, deplores and describes the ravages wrought by time, and still more by man, and recurring once again to the scene of his first inspiration, bids farewell to the Roman empire among the ruins of the Capitol.

We have hitherto spoken in terms of warm, though perhaps not excessive eulogy of this great work. But praise would lack the force of moderation and equipoise, if allusion were not made to some of its defects. The pervading defect of it all has been already referred to in a preceding chapter—an inadequate conception of society as an organism, living and growing, like other organisms, according to special laws of its own. In these brilliant volumes on the Middle Ages, the special problems which that period suggests are not stated, far less solved; they are not even suspected. The feudal polity, the Catholic Church, the theocratic supremacy of the Popes, considered as institutions which the historian is called upon to estimate and judge; the gradual dissolution of both feudalism and Catholicism, brought

about by the spread of industry in the temporal order
and of science in the spiritual order, are not even
referred to.   Many more topics might be added to this
list of weighty omissions.   It would be needless to
say that no blame attaches to Gibbon for neglecting
views of history which had not emerged in his time, if
there were not persons who, forgetting the slow progress of knowledge, are apt to ascribe the defects of a
book to incompetence in its author.   If Gibbon's conception of the Middle Ages seems to us inadequate now,
it is because since his time our conceptions of society in
that and in all periods have been much enlarged.   We
may be quite certain that if Gibbon had had our experience, no one would have seen the imperfections of
particular sides of his work as we now have it more
clearly than he.

Laying aside, therefore, reflexions of this kind as
irrelevant and unjust, we may ask whether there are
any other faults which may fairly be found with him.
One must admit that there are.   After all, they are not
very important.

(1.) Striking as is his account of Justinian's reign,
it has two blemishes.   First, the offensive details about
the vices of Theodora.   Granting them to be well
authenticated, which they are not, it was quite unworthy of the author and his subject to soil his pages
with such a *chronique scandaleuse*.   The defence which he
sets up in his Memoirs, that he is " justified in painting
the manners of the times, and that the vices of Theodora
form an essential feature in the reign and character of
Justinian," cannot be admitted.   First, we are not sure
that the vices existed, and were not the impure inven-
tions of a malignant calumniator.   Secondly, Gibbon

is far from painting the manners of the time as a
moralist or an historian ; he paints them with a zest
for pruriency worthy of Bayle or Brantome. It was
an occasion for a wise scepticism to register grave
doubts as to the infamous stories of Procopius. A
rehabilitation of Theodora is not a theme calculated to
provoke enthusiasm, and is impossible besides from the
entire want of adequate evidence. But a thoughtful
writer would not have lost his time, if he referred to
the subject at all, in pointing out the moral impro-
bability of the current accounts. He might have
dwelt on the *unsupported* testimony of the only witness,
the unscrupulous Procopius, whom Gibbon himself con-
victs on another subject of flagrant mendacity. But
he would have been especially slow to believe that a
woman who had led the life of incredible profligacy
he has described, would, in consequence of " some
vision either of sleep or fancy," in which future
exaltation was promised to her, assume " like a
skilful actress, a more decent character, relieve her
poverty by the laudable industry of spinning wool,
and affect a life of chastity and solitude in a small
house, which she afterwards changed into a magnificent
temple." Magdalens have been converted, no doubt,
from immoral living, but not by considerations of
astute prudence suggested by day-dreams of imperial
greatness. Gibbon might have thought of the case
of Madame de Maintenon, and how her reputation
fared in the hands of the vindictive courtiers of
Versailles ; how a woman, cold as ice and pure as
snow, was freely charged with the most abhorrent vices
without an atom of foundation. But the truth probably is that he never thought of the subject seriously

at all, and that, yielding to a regrettable inclination, he copied his licentious Greek notes with little reluctance.

(2.) The character of Belisarius, enigmatical enough in itself, is made by him more enigmatical still. He concludes the forty first chapter, in which the great deeds of the conqueror of Italy and Africa, and the ingratitude with which Justinian rewarded his services, are set forth in strong contrast, with the inept remark that "Belisarius appears to be either below or above the character of a MAN." The grounds of the apparent meekness with which Belisarius supported his repeated disgraces cannot now be ascertained : but the motives of Justinian's conduct are not so difficult to find. As Finlay points out in his thoughtful history of Greece, Belisarius must have been a peculator on a large and dangerous scale. "Though he refused the Gothic throne and the empire of the West, he did not despise nor neglect wealth : he accumulated riches which could not have been acquired by any commander-in-chief amidst the wars and famines of the period, without rendering the military and civil administration subservient to his pecuniary profit. On his return from Italy he lived at Constantinople in almost regal splendour, and maintained a body of 7,000 cavalry attached to his household. In an empire where confiscation was an ordinary financial resource, and under a sovereign whose situation rendered jealousy only common prudence, it is not surprising that the wealth of Belisarius excited the imperial cupidity, and induced Justinian to seize great part of it " (*Greece under the Romans*, chap. 3). There is shrewd insight in this, and though we may regret that we cannot attain to more, it is better than leaving the subject with an unmeaning paradox.

M

It may be said generally that Gibbon has not done
justice to the services rendered to Europe by the Byzantine empire. In his crowded forty-eighth chapter, which
is devoted to the subject, he passes over events and
characters with such speed that his history in this part
becomes little more than a chronicle, vivid indeed, but
barren of thoughtful political views. His account of
the Isaurian period may be instanced among others as
an example of defective treatment. If we turn to the
judicious Finlay, we see what an immense but generally
unacknowledged debt Europe owes to the Greek empire.
The saving of Christendom from Mohammedan conquest
is too easily attributed to the genius of Charles Martel
and his brave Franks. The victory at Tours was
important no doubt, but almost a century previously
the followers of the prophet had been checked by
Heraclius; and their memorable repulse before Constantinople under the Isaurian Leo was the real barrier
opposed to their conquest of the West. It requires but
little reflection to see that without this brave resistance
to the Moslem invasion, the course of mediæval history
would have been completely changed. Next in time,
but hardly second in value to the services of the Greeks
at Marathon and Salamis, must be reckoned the services
of the Byzantine emperors in repelling the barbarians.
Such an important consideration as this should hardly
have escaped Gibbon.

Gibbon's account of Charlemagne is strangely inadequate. It is perhaps the only instance in his work
where he has failed to appreciate a truly great man,
and the failure is the more deplorable as it concerns
one of the greatest men who have ever lived. He did
not realise the greatness of the man, of his age, or of his

work. Properly considered, the eighth century is the
most important and memorable which Europe has ever
seen. During its course the geographical limits, the
ecclesiastical polity, and the feudal system within
and under which our western group of nations was
destined to live for five or six centuries, were pro-
visionally settled and determined. The wonderful
house of the Carolings, which produced no less than
five successive rulers of genius (of whom two had
extraordinary genius, Charles Martel and Charlemagne,
were the human instruments of this great work. The
Frankish Monarchy was hastening to ruin when they
saved it. Saxons in the East and Saracens in the South
were on the point of extinguishing the few surviving
embers of civilisation which still existed. The Bishop
of Rome was ready to fall a prey to the Lombards, and
the progressive papacy of Hildebrand and Innocent
ran imminent risk of being extirpated at its root.
Charles and his ancestors prevented these evils. Of
course it is open to any one to say that there were no
evils threatening, that Mohammedanism is as good as
Christianity, that the Papacy was a monstrous calamity,
that to have allowed Eastern Germany to remain pagan
and barbarous would have done no harm. The question cannot be discussed here. But every law of historic
equity compels us to admit that whether the result was
good or bad, the genius of men who could leave such
lasting impressions on the world as the Carolings did,
must have been exceptionally great. And this is what
Gibbon has not seen; he has not seen that, whether
their work was good or bad in the issue, it was colossal.
His tone in reference to Charlemagne is unworthy to a
degree. " Without injustice to his fame, I may discern

M 2

some blemishes in the sanctity and greatness of the
restorer of the Western Empire. Of his moral virtues,
chastity was not the most conspicuous." This from the
pen of Gibbon seems hardly serious. Again : " I touch
with reverence the laws of Charlemagne, so highly applauded by a respectable judge. They compose not a
system, but a series of occasional and minute edicts,
for the correction of abuses, the reformation of manners,
the economy of his farms, the care of his poultry, and
even the sale of his eggs." And yet Gibbon had read
the Capitularies. The struggle and care of the hero to
master in some degree the wide welter of barbarism
surging around him, he never recognised. It is a spot
on Gibbon's fame.

Dean Milman considers that Gibbon's account of the
Crusades is the least accurate and satisfactory chapter
in his history, and "that he has here failed in that
lucid arrangement which in general gives perspicuity
to his most condensed and crowded narratives." This
blame seems to be fully merited, if restricted to the
second of the two chapters which Gibbon has devoted to the Crusades. The fifty-eighth chapter, in
which he treats of the First Crusade, leaves nothing to
be desired. It is not one of his best chapters, though it is
quite up to his usually high level. But the fifty-ninth
chapter, it must be owned, is not only weak, but what
is unexampled elsewhere in him, confused and badly
written. It is not, as in the case of Charlemagne, a
question of imperfect appreciation of a great man or
epoch ; it is a matter of careless and slovenly presentation of a period which he had evidently mastered with
his habitual thoroughness, but, owing to the rapidity
with which he composed his last volume, he did not do

full justice to it. He says significantly in his Memoirs, that "he wished that a pause, an interval, had been allowed for a serious revisal" of the last three volumes, and there can be little doubt that this chapter was one of the sources of his regrets. It is in fact a mere tangle. The Second and the Third Crusades are so jumbled together, that it is only a reader who knows the subject very well who can find his way through the labyrinth. Gibbon seems at this point, a thing very unusual with him, to have become impatient with his subject, and to have wished to hurry over it. "A brief parallel," he says, "may save the repetition of a tedious narrative." The result of this expeditious method has been far from happy. It is the only occasion where Gibbon has failed in his usual high finish and admirable literary form.

Gibbon's style was at one period somewhat of a party question. Good Christians felt a scruple in discerning any merits in the style of a writer who had treated the martyrs of the early Church with so little ceremony and generosity. On the other hand, those whose opinions approached more or less to his, expatiated on the splendour and majesty of his diction. Archbishop Whately went out of his way in a note to his *Logic* to make a keen thrust at an author whom it was well to depreciate whenever occasion served. "His way of writing," he says, "reminds one of those persons who never dare look you full in the face." Such criticisms are out of date now. The faults of Gibbon's style are obvious enough, and its compensatory merits are not far to seek. No one can overlook its frequent tumidity and constant want of terseness. It lacks suppleness, ease, variety. It is not often distinguished by happy

selection of epithet, and seems to ignore all delicacy
of *nuance*. A prevailing grandiloquence, which easily
slides into pomposity, is its greatest blemish. The acute
Porson saw this and expressed it admirably. In the
preface to his letters to Archdeacon Travis, he says of
Gibbon, "Though his style is in general correct and
elegant, he sometimes ' draws out the thread of his ver-
bosity finer than the staple of his argument.' In
endeavouring to avoid vulgar terms he too frequently
dignifies trifles, and clothes common thoughts in a
splendid dress that would be rich enough for the noblest
ideas. In short we are too often reminded of that great
man, Mr. Prig, the auctioneer, whose manner was so
inimitably fine that he had as much to say on a ribbon
as on a Raphael." It seems as if Gibbon had taken the
stilted tone of the old French tragedy for his model,
rather than the crisp and nervous prose of the best
French writers. We are constantly offended by a
superfine diction lavished on barbarous chiefs and rough
soldiers of the Lower Empire, which almost reproduces
the high-flown rhetoric in which Corneille's and Racine's
characters address each other. Such phrases as the
" majesty of the throne," " the dignity of the purple,"
the " wisdom of the senate," recur with a rather jarring
monotony, especially when the rest of the narrative is
designed to show that there was no majesty nor dignity
nor wisdom involved in the matter. We feel that the
writer was thinking more of his sonorous sentence than
of the real fact. On the other hand, nothing but a want
of candour or taste can lead any one to overlook the
rare and great excellences of Gibbon's style. First of
all, it is singularly correct : a rather common merit now,
but not common in his day. But its sustained vigour

and loftiness will always be uncommon; above all its
rapidity and masculine length of stride are quite admirable. When he takes up his pen to describe a campaign,
or any great historic scene, we feel that we shall
have something worthy of the occasion, that we shall be
carried swiftly and grandly through it all, without the
suspicion of a breakdown of any kind being possible.
An indefinable stamp of weightiness is impressed on
Gibbon's writing; he has a baritone manliness which
banishes everthing small, trivial, or weak. When he
is eloquent (and it should be remembered to his credit
that he never affects eloquence, though he occasionally
affects dignity), he rises without effort into real grandeur.
On the whole we may say that his manner, with certain
manifest faults, is not unworthy of his matter, and the
praise is great.

It is not quite easy to give expression to another
feeling which is often excited in reading Gibbon.
It is somewhat of this kind, that it is more fitted to
inspire admiration than love or sympathy. Its merits
are so great, the mass of information it contains is so
stupendous, that all competent judges of such work feel
bound to praise it. Whether they like it in the same
degree, may be questioned. Among reading men and
educated persons it is not common—such is my experience—to meet with people who know their Gibbon well.
Superior women do not seem to take to him kindly,
even when there is no impediment on religious grounds.
Madame du Deffand, writing to Walpole, says, "I
whisper it to you, but I am not pleased with Mr. Gibbon's work. It is declamatory, oratorical . . . I lay it
aside without regret, and it requires an effort to take it
up again." Another of Walpole's correspondents, the

Countess of Ossory, seems to have made similar strictures. If we admit that women are less capable than
masculine scholars of doing justice to the strong side of
Gibbon, we may also acknowledge that they are better
fitted than men to appreciate and to be shocked by his
defective side, which is a prevailing want of moral
elevation and nobility of sentiment. His cheek rarely
flushes in enthusiasm for a good cause. The tragedy of
human life never seems to touch him, no glimpse of the
infinite ever calms and raises the reader of his pages.
Like nearly all the men of his day, he was of the earth
earthy, and it is impossible to get over the fact.

CHAPTER X.

GIBBON had now only about six months to live. He did not seem to have suffered by his rapid journey from Lausanne to London. During the summer which he spent with his friend Lord Sheffield, he was much as usual ; only his friend noticed that his habitual dislike to motion appeared to increase, and he was so incapable of exercise that he was confined to the library and dining-room. "Then he joined Mr. F. North in pleasant arguments against exercise in general. He ridiculed the unsettled and restless disposition that summer, the most uncomfortable of all seasons, as he said, generally gives to those who have the use of their limbs." The true disciples of Epicurus are not always the least stout and stoical in the presence of irreparable evils.

After spending three or four months at Sheffield Place, he went to Bath to visit his stepmother, Mrs. Gibbon. His conduct to her through life was highly honourable to him. It should be remembered that her jointure, paid out of his father's decayed estate, was a great tax on his small income. In his efforts to improve his position by selling his landed property, Mrs. Gibbon seems to have been at times somewhat difficult to satisfy as regards the security of her interests. It was only

---

prudent on her part. But it is easy to see what a source of alienation and quarrel was here ready prepared, if both parties had not risen superior to sordid motives. There never seems to have been the smallest cloud between them. When one of his properties was sold he writes: "Mrs. Gibbon's jointure is secured on the Buriton estate, and her legal consent is requisite for the sale. Again and again I must repeat my hope that she is perfectly satisfied, and that the close of her life may not be embittered by suspicion, fear, or discontent. What new security does she prefer—the funds, a mortgage, or your land? At all events, she must be made easy." So Gibbon left town and lay at Reading on his road to Bath : here he passed about ten days with his stepmother, who was now nearly eighty years of age. "In mind and conversation she is just the same as twenty years ago," he writes to Lord Sheffield; "she has spirits, appetite, legs, and eyes, and talks of living till ninety. I can say from my heart, Amen." And in another letter, a few days later, he says : "A tête-à-tête of eight or nine hours every day is rather difficult to support; yet I do assure you that our conversation flows with more ease and spirit when we are alone, than when any auxiliaries are summoned to our aid. She is indeed a wonderful woman, and I think all her faculties of the mind stronger and more active than I have ever known them. . . . . I shall therefore depart next Friday, but I may possibly reckon without my host, as I have not yet apprised Mrs. G. of the term of my visit, and will certainly not quarrel with her for a short delay." He then went to Althorpe, and it is the last evidence of his touching a book—"exhausted the morning (of the 5th November) among the first editions of Cicero." Then he came to London, and in a few days was seized with the

illness which in a little more than two months put an
end to his life.

His malady was dropsy, complicated with other disorders. He had most strangely neglected a very dangerous symptom for upwards of thirty years, not only
having failed to take medical advice about it, but even
avoiding all allusion to it to bosom friends like Lord
Sheffield. But longer concealment was now impossible.
He sent for the eminent surgeon Farquhar (the same
who afterwards attended William Pitt), and he, together
with Cline, at once recognised the case as one of the utmost
gravity, though they did not say as much to the patient.
On Thursday, the 14th of November, he was tapped
and greatly relieved. He said he was not appalled by
the operation, and during its progress he did not lay
aside his usual good-humoured pleasantry. He was soon
out again, but only for a few days, and a fortnight
after another tapping was necessary. Again he went
out to dinners and parties, which must have been
most imprudent at his age and in his state. But
he does not seem to have acted contrary to medical
advice. He was very anxious to meet the prime
minister, William Pitt, with whom he was not acquainted, though he must have seen him in old days in
the House. He saw him twice; once at Eden Farm
for a whole day, and was much gratified, we are told.
At last he got to what he called his home—the house of
his true and devoted friend, Lord Sheffield. "But,"
says the latter, whose narrative of his friend's last
illness is marked by a deep and reserved tenderness
that does him much honour, "this last visit to
Sheffield Place became far different from any he had
ever made before. That ready, cheerful, various and
illuminating conversation which we had before admired

in him, was not always to be found in the library or the
drawing-room. He moved with difficulty, and retired
from company sooner than he had been used to do. On
the 23rd of December his appetite began to fail him. He
observed to me that it was a very bad sign *with him*
when he could not eat his breakfast, which he had done
at all times very heartily ; and this seems to have been
the strongest expression of apprehension that he was
ever observed to utter." He soon became too ill to
remain beyond the reach of the highest medical advice.
On the 7th of January, 1794, he left a houseful of company
and friends for his lodgings in St. James's Street. On
arriving he sent the following note to Lord Sheffield, the
last lines he ever wrote :—

"St. James's, Four o'Clock, Tuesday.

"This date says everything. I was almost killed
between Sheffield Place and East Grinstead by hard,
frozen, long, and cross ruts, that would disgrace the
approach of an Indian wigwam. The rest was somewhat less painful, and I reached this place half dead,
but not seriously feverish or ill. I found a dinner
invitation from Lord Lucan ; but what are dinners to
me ? I wish they did not know of my departure. I
catch the flying post. What an effort ! Adieu till
Thursday or Friday."

The end was not far off. On the 13th of January he
underwent another operation, and, as usual, experienced
much relief. " His spirits continued good. He talked
of passing his time at houses which he had often frequented with great pleasure—the Duke of Devonshire's,
Mr. Craufurd's, Lord Spencer's, Lord Lucan's, Sir Ralph
Payne's, Mr. Batt's." On the 14th of January " he
saw some company—Lady Lucan and Lady Spencer—

and thought himself well enough to omit the opium draught which he had been used to take for some time. He slept very indifferently; before nine the next morning he rose, but could not eat his breakfast. However, he appeared tolerably well, yet complained at times of a pain in his stomach. At one o'clock he received a visit of an hour from Madame de Sylva; and at three, his friend, Mr. Craufurd, of Auchinames (whom he always mentioned with particular regard), called, and stayed with him till past five o'clock. They talked, as usual, on various subjects; and twenty hours before his death Mr. Gibbon happened to fall into a conversation not uncommon with him, on the probable duration of his life. He said that he thought himself a good life for ten, twelve, or perhaps twenty years. About six he ate the wing of a chicken and drank three glasses of Madeira. After dinner he became very uneasy and impatient, complained a good deal, and appeared so weak that his servant was alarmed.

"During the evening he complained much of his stomach, and of a feeling of nausea. Soon after nine, he took his opium draught and went to bed. About ten he complained of much pain, and desired that warm napkins might be applied to his stomach. He almost incessantly expressed a sense of pain till about four o'clock in the morning, when he said he found his stomach much easier. About seven the servant asked whether he should send for Mr. Farquhar. He answered, No; that he was as well as the day before. At about half-past eight he got out of bed, and said he was 'plus adroit' than he had been for three months past, and got into bed again without assistance, better than usual. About nine he said he would rise. The servant, however, persuaded him to remain in bed till Mr. Farquhar, who was

expected at eleven, should come. Till about that hour
he spoke with great facility. Mr. Farquhar came at the
time appointed, and he was then visibly dying. When
the *valet-de-chambre* returned, after attending Mr.
Farquhar out of the room, Mr. Gibbon said, 'Pourquoi
est ce que vous me quittez?' This was about half-past
eleven. At twelve he drank some brandy and water
from a teapot, and desired his favourite servant to stay
with him. These were the last words he pronounced
articulately. To the last he preserved his senses; and
when he could no longer speak, his servant having asked
a question, he made a sign to show that he understood
him. He was quite tranquil, and did not stir, his eyes
half shut. About a quarter before one he ceased to
breathe." He wanted just eighty-three days of fifty-
seven years of age.

Thus, in consequence of his own strange self-neglect
and imprudence, was extinguished one of the most
richly-stored minds that ever lived. Occurring when it
did, so near the last summons, Gibbon's prospective hope
of continued life "for ten, twelve, or twenty years" is
harshly pathetic, and full of that irony which mocks
the vain cares of men. But, truly, his forecast was not
irrational if he had not neglected ordinary precautions.
In spite of his ailments he felt full, and was full, of life,
when he was cut off. We cannot be sure if lengthened
days would have added much to his work already
achieved. There is hardly a parallel case in literature
of the great powers of a whole life being so concentrated
on one supreme and magnificent effort. Yet, if he had
lived to 1804, or as an extreme limit, to 1814, we should
have been all gainers. In the first place, he certainly
would have finished his admirable autobiography. We
cannot imagine what he would have made of it, judging

from the fragment which exists.   And yet that fragment is almost a masterpiece.   But his fertile mind
had other schemes in prospect ; and what such a diligent worker would have done with a decade or two more
of years it is impossible to say, except that it is certain
they would not have been wasted.   The extinction of a
real mind is ever an irreparable loss.

As it was, he went to his rest after one of the greatest
victories ever achieved in his own field of humane letters,
and lived long enough to taste the fruits of his toil.   He
was never puffed up, but soberly and without arrogance
received his laurels.   His unselfish zeal and haste to
console his bereaved friend showed him warm and loving
to the last ; and we may say that his last serious effort
was consecrated to the genius of pious friendship.

In 1796, two years after Gibbon's death, Lord Sheffield published two quarto volumes of the historian's
miscellaneous works.   They have been republished in
one thick octavo, and many persons suppose that it contains the whole of the posthumous works ; not unnatu-
rally, as a fraudulent statement on the title-page,
" complete in one volume," is well calculated to produce
that impression.   But in 1814 Lord Sheffield issued a
second edition in five volumes octavo, containing much
additional matter, which additional matter was again
published in a quarto form, no doubt for the convenience
of the purchasers of the original quarto edition.

Of the posthumous works, the Memoirs are by far the
most important portion.   Unfortunately, they were left
in a most unfinished state, and what we now read is
nothing else than a mosaic put together by Lord Sheffield from *six* different sketches.   Next to the Memoirs
are the journals and diaries of his studies.   As a picture
of Gibbon's method, zeal, and thoroughness in the

pursuit of knowledge, they are of the highest interest.
But they refer to an early period of his studies, long
previous to the concentration of his mind on his great
work, and one would like to know whether they present
the best selection that might have been made from these
records. It is interesting to follow Gibbon in his perusal
of Homer and Juvenal at five-and-twenty. But one
would much like to be admitted to his study when he
was a far riper scholar, and preparing for or writing the
Decline and Fall. Lord Sheffield positively prohibited,
by a clause in his will, any further publication of the
Gibbon papers, and although Dean Milman was permitted to see them, it was with the express understanding that none of their contents should be divulged.
After the Memoirs and the journals, the most interesting
portion of the miscellaneous works are *The Antiquities
of the House of Brunswick*, which in their present form
are merely the preparatory sketch of a large work. It
is too imperfect to allow us to judge of what Gibbon
even designed to make of it. But it contains some masterly pages, and the style in many places seems more
nervous and supple than that of the *Decline and Fall.*
For instance, this account of Albert Azo the Second :—

"Like one of his Tuscan ancestors Azo the Second was distinguished among the princes of Italy by the epithet of the
Rich. The particulars of his rentroll cannot now be ascertained.
An occasional though authentic deed of investiture enumerates
eighty-three fiefs or manors which he held of the empire in
Lombardy and Tuscany, from the Marquisate of Este to the
county of Luni ; but to these possessions must be added the
lands which he enjoyed as the vassal of the Church, the ancient
patrimony of Otbert (the terra Obertenga) in the counties of
Arezzo, Pisa, and Lucca, and the marriage portion of his first
wife, which, according to the various readings of the manuscripts,
may be computed either at twenty or two hundred thousand

English acres. If such a mass of landed property were now accumulated on the head of an Italian nobleman, the annual revenue might satisfy the largest demands of private luxury or avarice, and the fortunate owner would be rich in the improvement of agriculture, the manufactures of industry, the refinement of taste, and the extent of commerce. But the barbarism of the eleventh century diminished the income and aggravated the expense of the Marquis of Este. In a long series of war and anarchy, man and the works of man had been swept away, and the introduction of each ferocious and idle stranger had been overbalanced by the loss of five or six perhaps of the peaceful industrious natives. The mischievous growth of vegetation, the frequent inundations of the rivers were no longer checked by the vigilance of labour ; the face of the country was again covered with forests and morasses ; of the vast domains which acknowledged Azo for their lord, the far greater part was abandoned to the beasts of the field, and a much smaller portion was reduced to the state of constant and productive husbandry. An adequate rent may be obtained from the skill and substance of a free tenant who fertilizes a grateful soil, and enjoys the security and benefit of a long lease. But faint is the hope and scanty is the produce of those harvests which are raised by the reluctant toil of peasants and slaves condemned to a bare subsistance and careless of the interests of a rapacious master. If his granaries are full, his purse is empty, and the want of cities or commerce, the difficulty of finding or reaching a market, obliges him to consume on the spot a part of his useless stock, which cannot be exchanged for merchandise or money. . . . The entertainment of his vassals and soldiers, their pay and rewards, their arms and horses, surpassed the measure of the most oppressive tribute, and the destruction which he inflicted on his neighbours was often retaliated on his own lands. The costly elegance of palaces and gardens was superseded by the laborious and expensive construction of strong castles on the summits of the most inaccessible rocks, and some of these, like the fortress of Canossa in the Apennine, were built and provided to sustain a three years' siege against a royal army. But his defence in this world was less burdensome to a wealthy lord than his salvation in the next ; the demands of his chapel, his priests, his

N

alms, his offerings, his pilgrimages were incessantly renewed ;
the monastery chosen for his sepulchre was endowed with his
fairest possessions, and the naked heir might often complain
that his father's sins had been redeemed at too high a price.
The Marquis Azo was not exempt from the contagion of the
times ; his devotion was animated and inflamed by the
frequent miracles that were performed in his presence ; and the
monks of Vangadizza, who yielded to his request the arm of a
dead saint, were not ignorant of the value of that inestimable
jewel.   After satisfying the demands of war and superstition he
might appropriate the rest of his revenue to use and pleasure.
But the Italians of the eleventh century were imperfectly skilled
in the liberal and mechanical arts ; the objects of foreign luxury
were furnished at an exorbitant price by the merchants of Pisa
and Venice ; and the superfluous wealth which could not
purchase the real comforts of life, were idly wasted on some
rare occasions of vanity and pomp.   Such were the nuptials of
Boniface, Duke or Marquis of Tuscany, whose family was long
after united with that of Azo by the marriage of their children.
These nuptials were celebrated on the banks of the Mincius,
which the fancy of Virgil has decorated with a more beautiful
picture.   The princes and people of Italy were invited to the
feasts, which continued three months ; the fertile meadows,
which are intersected by the slow and winding course of the
river, were covered with innumerable tents, and the bridegroom
displayed and diversified the scenes of his proud and tasteless
magnificence.   All the utensils of the service were of silver,
and his horses were shod with plates of the same metal, loosely
nailed and carelessly dropped, to indicate his contempt of riches.
An image of plenty and profusion was expressed in the banquet ;
the most delicious wines were drawn in buckets from the well ;
and the spices of the East were ground in water-mills like
common flour.   The dramatic and musical arts were in the
rudest state ; but the Marquis had summoned the most popular
singers, harpers, and buffoons to exercise their talents in this
splendid theatre.   After this festival I might remark a singular
gift of this same Boniface to the Emperor Henry III., a chariot
and oxen of solid silver, which were designed only as a vehicle
for a hogshead of vinegar.   If such an example should seem

above the imitation of Azo himself, the Marquis of Este was at least superior in wealth and dignity to the vassals of his compeer. One of these vassals, the Viscount of Mantua, presented the German monarch with one hundred falcons and one hundred bay horses, a grateful contribution to the pleasures of a royal sportsman. In that age the proud distinction between the nobles and princes of Italy was guarded with jealous ceremony. The Viscount of Mantua had never been seated at the table of his immediate lord ; he yielded to the invitation of the Emperor ; and a stag's skin filled with pieces of gold was graciously accepted by the Marquis of Tuscany as the fine of his presumption.

" The temporal felicity of Azo was crowned by the long possession of honour and riches; he died in the year 1097, aged upwards of an hundred years ; and the term of his mortal existence was almost commensurate with the lapse of the eleventh century. The character as well as the situation of the Marquis of Este rendered him an actor in the revolutions of that memorable period ; but time has cast a veil over the virtues and vices of the man, and I must be content to mark some of the eras, the milestones of his which measure the extent and intervals of the vacant way. Albert Azo the Second was no more than seventeen when he first drew the sword of rebellion and patriotism, when he was involved with his grandfather, his father, and his three uncles in a common proscription. In the vigour of his manhood, about his fiftieth year, the Ligurian Marquis governed the cities of Milan and Genoa as the minister of Imperial authority. He was upwards of seventy when he passed the Alps to vindicate the inheritance of Maine for the children of his second marriage. He became the friend and servant of Gregory VII., and in one of his epistles that ambitious pontiff recommends the Marquis Azo, as the most faithful and best beloved of the Italian princes, as the proper channel through which a king of Hungary might convey his petitions to the apostolic throne. In the mighty contest between the crown and the mitre, the Marquis Azo and the Countess Matilda led the powers of Italy. And when the standard of St. Peter was displayed, neither the age of the one nor the sex of the other could detain them from the field. With these two affectionate clients the Pope maintained his station in the fortress of Canossa, while

the Emperor, barefoot on the frozen ground, fasted and prayed
three days at the foot of the rock ; they were witnesses to the
abject ceremony of the penance and pardon of Henry IV. ; and
in the triumph of the Church a patriot might foresee the de-
liverance of Italy from the German yoke. At the time of this
event the Marquis of Este was above fourscore ; but in the
twenty following years he was still alive and active amidst the
revolutions of peace and war. The last act which he subscribed is dated above a century after his birth ; and in that
the venerable chief possesses the command of his faculties, his
family, and his fortune. In this rare prerogative the longevity
of Albert Azo the Second stands alone. Nor can I remember
in the *authentic* annals of mortality a single example of a king
or prince, of a statesman or general, of a philosopher or poet,
whose life has been extended beyond the period of a hundred
years. . . . Three approximations which will not hastily be
matched have distinguished the present century, Aurungzebe,
Cardinal Fleury, and Fontenelle. Had a fortnight more been
given to the philosopher, he might have celebrated his secular
festival ; but the lives and labours of the Mogul king and the
French minister were terminated before they had accomplished
their ninetieth year."

Then follow several striking and graceful pages on
Lucrezia Borgia and Renée of France, Duchess of
Ferrara. The following description of the University
of Padua and the literary tastes of the house of Este
is all that we can give here :—

" An university had been founded at Padua by the house of
Este, and the scholastic rust was polished away by the revival
of the literature of Greece and Rome. The studies of Ferrara
were directed by skilful and eloquent professors, either natives
or foreigners. The ducal library was filled with a valuable
collection of manuscripts and printed books, and as soon as
twelve new plays of Plautus had been found in Germany, the
Marquis Lionel of Este was impatient to obtain a fair and
faithful copy of that ancient poet. Nor were these elegant
pleasures confined to the learned world. Under the reign of

Hercules I. a wooden theatre at a moderate cost of a thousand crowns was constructed in the largest court of the palace, the scenery represented some houses, a seaport and a ship, and the *Menechmi* of Plautus, which had been translated into Italian by the Duke himself, was acted before a numerous and polite audience. In the same language and with the same success the *Amphytrion* of Plautus and the *Eunuchus* of Terence were successively exhibited. And these classic models, which formed the taste of the spectators, excited the emulation of the poets of the age. For the use of the court and theatre of Ferrara, Ariosto composed his comedies, which were often played with applause, which are still read with pleasure. And such was the enthusiasm of the new arts that one of the sons of Alphonso the First did not disdain to speak a prologue on the stage. In the legitimate forms of dramatic composition the Italians have not excelled ; but it was in the court of Ferrara that they invented and refined the *pastoral comedy*, a romantic Arcadia which violates the truth of manners and the simplicity of nature, but which commands our indulgence by the elaborate luxury of eloquence and wit. The *Aminta* of Tasso was written for the amusement and acted in the presence of Alphonso the Second, and his sister Leonora might apply to herself the language of a passion which disordered the reason without clouding the genius of her poetical lover. Of the numerous imitations, the *Pastor Fido* of Guarini, which alone can vie with the fame and merit of the original, is the work of the Duke's secretary of state. It was exhibited in a private house in Ferrara. . . . . The father of the Tuscan muses, the sublime but unequal Dante, had pronounced that Ferrara was never honoured with the name of a poet ; he would have been astonished to behold the chorus of bards, of melodious swans (their own allusion), which now peopled the banks of the Po. In the court of Duke Borso and his successor, Boyardo Count Scandiano, was respected as a noble, a soldier, and a scholar : his vigorous fancy first celebrated the loves and exploits of the paladin Orlando ; and his fame has been preserved and eclipsed by the brighter glories and continuation of his work. Ferrara may boast that on classic ground Ariosto and Tasso lived and sung ; that the lines of the *Orlando Furioso*, the

Gierusalemme Liberata were inscribed in everlasting characters under the eye of the First and Second Alphonso.   In a period of near three thousand years, five great epic poets have arisen in the world, and it is a singular prerogative that two of the five should be claimed as their own by a short age and a petty state."

It perhaps will be admitted that if the style of these passages is less elaborate than that of the *Decline and Fall*, the deficiency, if it is one, is compensated by greater ease and lightness of touch.

It may be interesting to give a specimen of Gibbon's French style.   His command of that language was not inferior to his command of his native idiom.   One might even be inclined to say that his French prose is controlled by a purer taste than his English prose.   The following excerpt, describing the Battle of Morgarten, will enable the reader to judge.   It is taken from his early unfinished work on the History of the Swiss Republic, to which reference has already been made (p. 59) :—

" Léopold était parti de Zug vers le milieu de la nuit.   Il se flattait d'occuper sans résistance le défilé de Morgarten qui ne perçait qu'avec difficulté entre le lac Aegré et le pied d'une montagne escarpée.   Il marchait à la tête de sa gendarmerie. Une colonne profond d'infanterie le suivait de près, et les uns et les autres se promettaient une victoire facile si les paysans osaient se présenter à leur rencontre.   Ils étaient à peine entrés dans un chemin rude et étroit, et qui ne permettait qu'à trois ou quatre de marcher de front, qu'ils se sentirent accablés d'une grêle de pierres et de traits.   Rodolphe de Reding, landamman de Schwitz et général des Confédérés, n'avait oublié aucun des avantages que lui offrit la situation des lieux.   Il avait fait couper des rochers énormes, qui en s'ébranlant dès qu'on retirait les faibles appuis qui les retenaient encore, se détachaient du sommet de la montaigne et se précipitaient avec un bruit

affreux sur les bataillons serrés des Autrichiens. Déjà les
chevaux s'éffrayaient, les rangs se confondaient, et le désordre
égarait le courage et le rendait inutile, lorsque les Suisses de-
scendirent de la montagne en poussant de grands cris. Ac-
coutumés à poursuivre le chamois sur les bords glissants des
précipices, ils couraient d'un pas assuré au milieu des neiges.
Ils étaient armés de grosses et pesantes hallebardes, auxquelles
le fer le mieux trempé ne résistait point. Les soldats de Léopold
chancelants et découragés cédèrent bientôt aux efforts désespérés
d'une troupe qui combattait pour tout ce qu'il y a de plus cher
aux hommes. L'Abbé d'Einsidlen, premier auteur de cette
guerre malheureuse, et le comte Henri de Montfort, donnèrent
les premiers l'exemple de la fuite. Le désordre devint général,
le carnage fut affreux, et les Suisses se livraient au plaisir de
la vengeance. A neuf heures du matin la bataille était gagnée.
. . . . Un grand nombre d'Autrichiens se précipitant les uns
sur les autres, cherchèrent vainement dans le lac un asyle contre
la fureur de leurs ennemis. Ils y périrent presque tous.
Quinze cents hommes restèrent sur le champ de bataille. Ils
étaient pour la plupart de la gendarmerie, qu'une valeur malheureuse et une armure pesante arrêtaient dans un lieu où
l'un et l'autre leur étaient inutiles. Longtemps après l'on
s'apercevait dans toutes les provinces voisines que l'élite de
la noblesse avait péri dans cette fatale journée. L'infanterie
beaucoup moins engagée dans le défilé, vit en tremblant la
défaite des chevaliers qui passaient pour invincibles, et dont les
escadrons effrayés se renversaient sur elle. Elle s'arrêta, voulut
se retirer, et dans l'instant cette retraite devint une fuite hon-
teuse. Sa perte fut assez peu considérable, mais les historiens
de la nation ont conservé la mémoire de cinquante braves
Zuriquois dont on trouva les rangs couchés morts sur la place.
Léopold lui-même fut entrainé par la foule qui le portait du
côté de Zug. On le vit entrer dans sa ville de Winterthur. La
frayeur, la honte et l'indignation étaient encore peintes sur son
front. Dès que la victoire se fut déclarée en faveur des Suisses,
ils s'assemblèrent sur le champ de bataille, s'embrassèrent en
versant des larmes d'allégresse, et remercièrent Dieu de la grace
qu'il venait de leur faire, et qui ne leur avait coûté que quatorze
de leurs compagnons."

His familiar letters and a number of essays, chiefly
written in youth, form the remainder of the miscellaneous works. Of the letters, some have been quoted
in this volume, and the reader can form his own judgment of them. Of the small essays we may say that
they augment, if it is possible, one's notion of Gibbon's
laborious diligence and thoroughness in the field of
historic research, and confirm his title to the character
of an intrepid student.

The lives of scholars are proverbially dull, and that of
Gibbon is hardly an exception to the rule. In the case
of historians, the protracted silent labour of preparation,
followed by the conscientious exposition of knowledge
acquired, into which the intrusion of the writer's per-
sonality rarely appears to advantage, combine to give
prominence to the work achieved, and to throw into
the background the author who achieves it. If indeed
the historian, forsaking his high function and austere
reserve, succumbs to the temptations that beset his
path, and turns history into political pamphlet, poetic
rhapsody, moral epigram, or garish melodrama, he may
become conspicuous to a fault at the expense of his
work. Gibbon avoided these seductions. If the *Decline
and Fall* has no superior in historical literature, it is
not solely in consequence of Gibbon's profound learning,
wide survey, and masterly grasp of his subject. With
wise discretion, he subordinated himself to his task. The
life of Gibbon is the less interesting, but his work
remains monumental and supreme.

LONDON : R. CLAY, SONS, AND TAYLOR, PRINTERS.